Photo by Gerry Goodstein

Deborah Hedwall, John De Vries and Dennis Boutsikaris in a scene from the
Manhattan Theatre Club production of "Sight Unseen." Set design by James Youmans.

SIGHT UNSEEN

BY DONALD MARGULIES

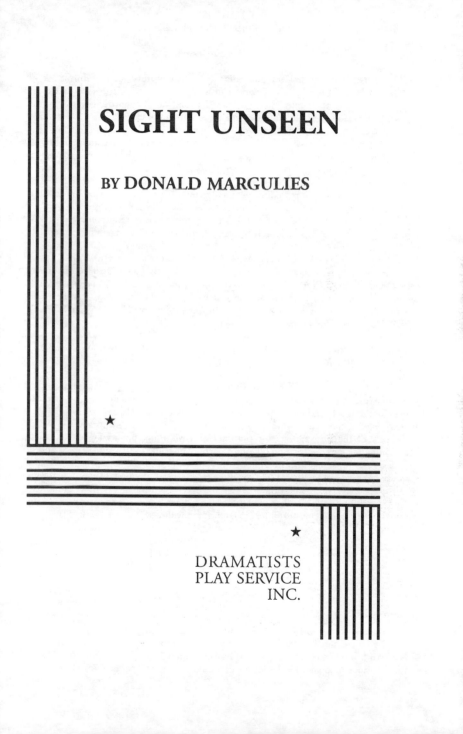

DRAMATISTS
PLAY SERVICE
INC.

SPECIAL NOTE

SPECIAL NOTE ON ORIGINAL MUSIC

2

This play is for
Jonathan Alper
(1950-1991)
and
Laura Kuckes
(1961-1990)

ACKNOWLEDGMENTS

The author wishes to acknowledge the following people for their insight and hard work which contributed to the development and success of *Sight Unseen:* all the folks at South Coast Rep, particularly Jerry Patch, Elizabeth Norment, Stephen Rowe, Randy Oglesby, Sabina Weber, Michael Roth, Cliff Faulkner, Daniel Reichert, Kamella Tate, Kris Logan, Anni Long and Jarion Monroe; David Kranes and the actors at the Sundance Playwrights Conference who worked on an early version of the play, most notably Evan Handler, Kevin Kling, Mia Dillon, Daniel Jenkins and Kathy Hiler; New Dramatists; Kate Nelligan, Anthony Heald, Peter Friedman, Wendy Makkena; Bruce Whitacre, Kate Loewald and everybody who worked on the Manhattan Theatre Club production, most especially Michael Bloom, Dennis Boutsikaris, Deborah Hedwall, Laura Linney, Jon DeVries and Lou Liberatore. Special thanks also to my wife, Lynn Street.

SIGHT UNSEEN received its world premiere at South Coast Repertory (Martin Benson, Artistic Director; David Emmes, Producing Artistic Director), in Costa Mesa, California, on September 17, 1991. It was directed by Michael Bloom; the set design was by Cliff Faulkner; the costume design was by Ann Bruice; the lighting design was by Tom Ruzika and the music was by Michael Roth. The cast was as follows:

JONATHAN WAXMAN .... Stephen Rowe
NICK .... Randy Oglesby
PATRICIA .... Elizabeth Norment
GRETE .... Sabina Weber

SIGHT UNSEEN began performances at Manhattan Theatre Club (Lynne Meadow, Artistic Director; Barry Grove, Managing Director) on January 7, and moved to the Orpheum Theatre on March 26, 1992, in New York City. It was directed by Michael Bloom; the set design was by James Youmans; the costume design was by Jess Goldstein; the lighting design was by Donald Holder and the music was by Michael Roth. The cast was as follows:

JONATHAN WAXMAN .... Dennis Boutsikaris
NICK .... Jon De Vries
PATRICIA .... Deborah Hedwall
GRETE .... Laura Linney

CHARACTERS

JONATHAN, 35-40
PATRICIA, 35-40
NICK, 40s
GRETE, 25-30

Jonathan and Patricia are American; Nick is English. Grete is German; her English is excellent, if accented. Jonathan has maintained his working-class Brooklyn accent; Nick's rural, working-class speech finds its way into his University accent, particularly when he's been drinking; and Patricia's dialect suggests that of an expatriate New Yorker living in England.

SCENES

Act One
1. A cold farmhouse in Norfolk, England. The present.
2. An art gallery in London. Four days later.
3. The farmhouse. An hour before the start of Scene 1.
4. A bedroom in Brooklyn. 15 years earlier.

Act Two
5. The farmhouse. A few hours after the end of Scene 1.
6. The art gallery. Continued from the end of Scene 2.
7. The farmhouse. A few hours after the end of Scene 5.
8 . A painting studio in an art college. New York State. 17 years earlier.

A turntable should ideally be used to ensure quick transitions between the four discrete settings.

The play is performed with an intermission after Scene 4.

6

SIGHT UNSEEN

ACT ONE

Scene 1

Lights up: The kitchen of a cold farmhouse in England. Dusk. Jonathan, overnight bag on his shoulder, stands at the open door. Nick is eating a hard roll.

JONATHAN.   You must be Nick.

NICK.   Mm.

JONATHAN.   Jonathan Waxman. *(He extends his hand. Nick doesn't shake it, but takes a bite of his roll instead.)* Is Patricia...? *(Nick shakes his head.)* Oh. You *were* expecting me?

NICK.   Mm.

JONATHAN.   *(Meaning, Where is...?)* Patricia...?

NICK.   A lamb roast.

JONATHAN.   Ah. Well! Nick! Nice to meet you. *(Nick says nothing. A beat.)* I left the car right outside. That alright? *(Nick looks out the door, shrugs.)* 'Cause I'll move it.

NICK.   No no. *(A beat.)*

JONATHAN.   Uh, I think I'm kind of freezing. You mind if I — *(Nick gestures for him to come in.)* Thanks. *(A beat.)* I made really good time, by the way. Left London 'round one; not bad, huh? *(Nick shrugs. A beat.)* Her directions were really good Patricia. *(A beat.)* Boy, this driving on the wrong side of the road stuff! — Ever drive in America? *(Nick shakes his head.)* Ever *been* to America? *(Nick shakes his head again.)* Uh huh, well it's *weird* cars coming at you like that. A simple thing like the way you perceive the flow of traffic, the way you're used

7

to seeing, gets challenged here, it all gets inverted. You've got to keep reminding yourself, over and over, remember what side of the road you're on. 'Cause all you need's to zone out for one second on the M4 and that's it, you're fucken wrapped in twisted metal. *(Nick just looks at him. A beat.)* Will she be long Patricia?

NICK.   God, I hope not.

JONATHAN.   Oh, I'm sorry, am I interrupting something?

NICK.   *(Gestures to a room)* Well ...

JONATHAN.   Please. Do what you have to do. I want to hear all about your work, though.

NICK.   Hm?

JONATHAN.   Your work. I really want to hear about it.

NICK.   Oh.

JONATHAN.   Archeology's one of those things I've always found fascinating, but I don't know much about it.

NICK.   Well, I ...

JONATHAN.   Not now. Whenever. Over dinner. I brought you some good wine; we should drink it. *(Takes out bottles of wine.)* Maybe later I'll get you to show me the dig you're working on.

NICK.   Uh ...

JONATHAN.   No, really, I'd like to see it. Hey, I know how obnoxious it is when people say they want to see my studio and then I show them and they're not really into it?, all they're thinking about is *after*, telling their friends they were there? No, I mean it, I'd really love to see it.

NICK.   It's.... It's rather dull.

JONATHAN.   I'm sure it isn't. What are you working on right now?

NICK.   *(A beat)* A Roman latrine. *(A beat. Patricia enters wearing a bulky sweater and carrying a bag bursting with groceries.)*

PATRICIA.   Well! You're here!

JONATHAN.   *(Over "You're here!")* Hi. Yeah. *(She moves around the room, unpacks groceries, prepares dinner.)*

PATRICIA.   Fancy car.

JONATHAN.   Rented. *You* know. What the hell.

PATRICIA.   Must be fun whipping round these country roads

8

in a thing like that.

JONATHAN. Yeah, as a matter of fact I was just telling Nick ...

NICK. Um ...

PATRICIA. What. *(He gestures to his office.)* Go. *(Nick hesitates, goes. A beat.)* He has work. *(Jonathan nods. A beat.)* So. Arrived in one piece I see.

JONATHAN. Your directions ...

PATRICIA. What.

JONATHAN. Excellent. Just terrific.

PATRICIA. Oh, good. I'm glad you liked them.

JONATHAN. Great spot.

PATRICIA. Yeah? Looks like a lot of mud most of the time. *(Pause.)*

JONATHAN. Good to see you, Patty.

PATRICIA. Is it? Well, good. *(Pause.)*

JONATHAN. So you got a lamb roast?

PATRICIA. Ground veal, actually. It was on special. I've become quite a resourceful little cook over here, you know. *(Nick returns, gets a bottle of scotch, gestures offstage, exits.)* Nick is painfully shy. Was he shy with you?

JONATHAN. *(Lying.)* Nick? No. *(A beat.)* So you've become a good cook you said?

PATRICIA. I didn't say good, I said resourceful. No one's a good cook here, so no one notices. Stews are the answer, I've discovered. The meat quality is so awful, you stew the stuff for hours till it all falls apart and it's unrecognizable as meat. Bet you can't wait for dinner, hm? *(She puts on water for tea, etc.)*

JONATHAN. Mmm. Can I help with anything?

PATRICIA. *(Over "with anything?")* No. Sit. Pretend you're comfortable. Take off your coat.

JONATHAN. *(Meaning the cold.)* No, I'll keep it if you don't mind ...

PATRICIA. It's so funny having Americans visit, watching their teeth chatter.

JONATHAN. I think it's warmer out*side*.

PATRICIA. Probably. You get used to the cold and the

9

damp, strangely enough. You get used to anything.

JONATHAN. You've kept your accent.

PATRICIA. For the most part. You'll notice little things here and there.

JONATHAN. It struck me on the phone; I thought by now you'd sound totally ...

PATRICIA. I don't know, I like sounding American. It works to my advantage, really. You have no idea how hard it is being a woman running an excavation.

JONATHAN. I'll bet.

PATRICIA. The sexism here.... If you think the *States* are bad.... Being an *American* woman gives me license to be rude, aggressive, demanding. It comes in handy.

JONATHAN. Don't you ever miss it?

PATRICIA. What?

JONATHAN. Home.

PATRICIA. This is my home.

JONATHAN. What, you don't miss Disneyland, or the Grand Canyon, or Zabar's?

PATRICIA. No.

JONATHAN. You don't miss Zabar's? Now I know you're full of it.

PATRICIA. I don't. I don't get choked up when I see the flag, or Woody Allen movies. I've stopped reading about politics. Reagan, Bush, they're interchangeable. No, I prefer my bones and coins and petrified cherry pits.

JONATHAN. You must miss *some*thing. Insulated housing, *some*thing.

PATRICIA. No. I'm an expatriate now.

JONATHAN. An expatriate.

PATRICIA. Yes.

JONATHAN. Gee, I've never known an expatriate before, someone who could just turn their back ...

PATRICIA. On what. I've turned my back on what? America? V.C.R.s and microwaves? If that's what I've "turned my back on" ... We work hard here. It's not like the States. Everything is a struggle. It shows on our faces, on our hands. I haven't bought myself new clothes in years. We have to save

10

for everything. The electric fire started smoking?
JONATHAN.   Yeah...?
PATRICIA.   It'll be weeks before we can buy a new one.
Everything's a struggle. The weather is hard. Leisure is hard.
Sleep is hard.
JONATHAN.   Do you ever think about leaving?
PATRICIA.   God! What have I been saying! I like it!
JONATHAN.   Oh.
PATRICIA.   You're just like my mother! I *like* it here! I *like*
the struggle! I *like* surviving obstacles. Hell, I survived *you*,
didn't I. *(He reaches for her hand, she pulls away. Pause.)* Who
are you to talk about turning one's back.
JONATHAN.   What do you mean?
PATRICIA.   You with your shiksa wife in Vermont.
JONATHAN.   Upstate.
PATRICIA.   Whatever.
JONATHAN.   I don't understand. What does my wife have
to do ...
PATRICIA.   *(Over "have to do...")* You're an expatriate, too,
and you don't even know it.
JONATHAN.   How?
PATRICIA.   You made a choice. When you married your
wife, you married her world. Didn't you? You can't exist in
two worlds; you've got to turn your back on one of them.
JONATHAN.   I hadn't thought of it like that.
PATRICIA.   See? We're more alike than you thought. *(Pause.)*
God, when I think of all the angst, all the, what's the word?,
"cirrus"?
JONATHAN.   *Tsuris.*
PATRICIA.   After all the tsuris our young souls went
through.... Your wife should thank me.
JONATHAN.   You're right; she should.
PATRICIA.   I laid the groundwork. I was the pioneer.
JONATHAN.   Yeah.
PATRICIA.   The sacrificial shiksa.
JONATHAN.   You're looking beautiful, Patty.
PATRICIA.   Stop.
JONATHAN.   You are.

11

PATRICIA. I look fat.

JONATHAN. No.

PATRICIA. All the meat and potatoes, and nights at the pub. Don't look at me. I'm afraid this place is perfect for women like me, who've let themselves go.

JONATHAN. You haven't.

PATRICIA. We can blend right in with the mud.

JONATHAN. You look beautiful.

PATRICIA. And *you* look rich.

JONATHAN. I don't even. I'm the same old Jonathan.

PATRICIA. Don't be coy. You're rich and famous. How does it feel to be rich and famous?

JONATHAN. It's meaningless. Really.

PATRICIA. Oh, yeah, right.

JONATHAN. No, the whole scene is meaningless bullshit. You know that. It's all timing and luck.

PATRICIA. Timing and luck.

JONATHAN. Yeah. The party's over for me already; I'm not making now what I made two years ago.

PATRICIA. But you still have your millions to keep you company.

JONATHAN. The numbers don't mean anything. I mean, I'm not crying poverty or anything ...

PATRICIA. Oh! Well!

JONATHAN. My gallery takes fifty per cent. Okay? Remember that. Fifty. And then the government on top of that ...

PATRICIA. Don't you think you're protesting just a little too much?

JONATHAN. Okay, so maybe I've enjoyed a little recognition —

PATRICIA. "A little recognition"?! Jonathan! You're "it,"

JONATHAN. No, no, not anymore.

PATRICIA. *(Continuous.)* the cat's pajamas. You can't fool me. I read all about you in The *Times*.

JONATHAN. The New York *Times?* You read the New York *Times?* Hypocrite. You were just telling me how you ...

PATRICIA. *(Over "telling me how you ...")* My mother sent it to me.

JONATHAN. You talking about the Sunday Magazine piece?
Couple of years ago?
PATRICIA. "Jonathan Waxman: The Art Scene's New Visionary."
JONATHAN. Oh, please ...
PATRICIA. (*Overlap, laughs, then.*) Is that what it was?: "New
Visionary"?
JONATHAN. "Bad Boy or Visionary"?
PATRICIA. "Bad Boy or Visionary," excuse me.
JONATHAN. What do you want from me?
PATRICIA. Cover story and everything. Wow, Jonathan,
how'd you manage that? I was quite impressed. You on the
cover, the very model of messy, Jewish intensity.
JONATHAN. They shot me in my studio. That's how I look
when I'm working.
PATRICIA. I know how you look when you're working. (*They
look at one another. Pause.*) My mother's always sending me clippings about you.
JONATHAN. Oh, yeah? Why?
PATRICIA. I don't know, I'd say she's trying to tell me
something, wouldn't you? The *Vanity Fair* piece was fun.
"Charlatan or Genius?"
JONATHAN. I don't believe this.
PATRICIA. Every time she sends me something, I take it as
some sort of indictment, some sort of accusation: "*See what you
could've had? See what could've been yours if you weren't so crazy?*"
JONATHAN. Is that what *you* think or is that what *she*
think?
PATRICIA. Me? No. (*Pause.*) So tell me about your show.
How's it going in London? (*That English inflection slips in.*) Is
it going well?
JONATHAN. Yeah. Pretty much. Oh, I brought you a catalogue. (*Hands her one from his bag.*)
PATRICIA. Hefty.
JONATHAN. There are a couple of gaps I'm not too happy
about. Particularly in the early stuff. It's supposed to be a retrospective.
PATRICIA. A retrospective? At your age?

13

JONATHAN.   Are you kidding? I'm almost passe.

PATRICIA.   You know, I still have that very first painting you did of me, remember?

JONATHAN.   Of course I remember. Where is it?

PATRICIA.   Over the mantle. Go and see.

JONATHAN.   No shit. You didn't just haul it out of the attic, knowing I was coming?

PATRICIA.   There is no attic. And, no, Jonathan, I wouldn't do anything at this point to feed your ego. *(He goes to the doorway leading to the living room and sees his painting; it's like seeing a ghost. She watches him in silence while he looks at the painting.)*

JONATHAN.   Jesus. Look at that. I can't believe you saved it. How old could I have been? Twenty-two tops? *(She nods; a beat.)* You know? It's not bad. I threw out most of my student work years ago. I couldn't stand looking at anything. But this, this one's different. It's really not bad.

PATRICIA.   When do you open?

JONATHAN.   What? Oh. Tuesday. *(Re: the painting.)* Look at that: see what I was doing with the picture plane?, how it's sort of tipped? I didn't think I started doing that till like much later.

PATRICIA.   Nervous?

JONATHAN.   No. I don't know. What can I do? It's my first solo show outside of North America, okay?, my European debut.

PATRICIA.   Yeah...?

JONATHAN.   So the critics are salivating, I'm sure. Ready to chomp into me like their next Big Mac.

PATRICIA.   And what if they do?

JONATHAN.   I don't know, I can't worry about it. Press is press. Good or bad. My father, God!, my father *loved* seeing my name in print.

PATRICIA.   Oh, yeah?

JONATHAN.   *My* last name, after all, was *his* last name. Got such a kick out of it. Eight pages in the Sunday *Times*. He couldn't believe The New York *Times* could possibly have that much to say about *his* kid. "All these words," he said, "are about *you*? What is there to say about *you*?" *(She laughs.)* He was serious; he wasn't just teasing. Oh, he was teasing, too, but it threatened him. No, it did. It pointed up the fact that he could be my father and still not know a thing about me. Not have a clue. What did the fancy – schmancy art world see that he didn't? What were those big dirty paintings about, anyway? So then when all the hype started ...

PATRICIA.   "New visionary?"

JONATHAN.   Yeah, and that's very seductive in the beginning, I got to admit. Vindicating, even: "Ah ha! See? I *am* a genius. *Now* maybe my father will respect me." But it had the opposite effect on him. It didn't make him proud. It bewildered him. It alienated him. How could *he* have produced a "visionary?" It shamed him somehow, I can't explain.

PATRICIA.   How's he doing?

JONATHAN.   Oh. Didn't I tell you on the phone?

PATRICIA.   What.

JONATHAN.   He died.

PATRICIA.   Oh, no.

JONATHAN.   Right before I flew to London.

PATRICIA.   You mean last week?

JONATHAN.   What's today? Yeah, last Thursday it happened.

PATRICIA.   Oh, Jonathan.... What happened?

JONATHAN.   It was long in coming. Did I not mention this on the phone?

PATRICIA.   No.

JONATHAN.   Sorry, thought I did. Strange to think, four days ago I was in Flushing, Queens, burying my father under the Unisphere. *(Pause.)*

PATRICIA.   *He* was sweet to me, your Dad.

JONATHAN.   Yeah, I know.

PATRICIA.   What about shiva? Didn't you have to sit shiva?

JONATHAN.   There was no time.

PATRICIA.   Oh.

JONATHAN.   I mean, they were mounting the show.

PATRICIA.   Couldn't they have waited? I mean, your *father* ...

JONATHAN.   No. I had to be here. I mean, there was nothing more I could do; he was dead. What could I do?

15

PATRICIA.   I don't know.

JONATHAN.   It was good for me, getting away, I think. Therapeutic. Bobby's doing it, though, shiva. He wanted to. I don't know, I just couldn't. It didn't seem like the thing to do. It's like I'd been sitting shiva for him for fifteen years, since my mother. I'd done it already. *(A beat.)* I wasn't a very good son.

PATRICIA.   That's not true; I'm sure you made him very proud.

JONATHAN.   No no, that's not what I need to hear. I wasn't. *(A beat.)* I went to pack up my his house the other day? My parents' house? All his clothes, my old room, my mother's sewing machine, all those rooms of furniture. Strange being in a place where no one lives anymore.

PATRICIA.   I know; I do that for a living.

JONATHAN.   Yeah, I guess you do. Anyway, what I found was, he'd taken all the family pictures, everything that was in albums, shoved in drawers — hundreds of them — and covered an entire wall with them, floor to ceiling, side to side. I first saw it years ago, when he'd started. It was his Sistine Chapel; it took him years. He took my hand (I'll never forget this) he took my hand — he was beaming: *"You're* an artist," he said to me, *"you'll* appreciate this." He was so proud of himself I thought I was gonna cry. Proud and also in a strange way competitive?

PATRICIA.   Uh huh.

JONATHAN.   So, there was this wall. The Waxman family through the ages. Black-and-white, sepia, Kodachrome. My great-grandparents in the shtetl, my brother's baby pictures on top of my parents' courtship, me at my bar mitzvah. Well, it was kind of breathtaking. I mean, the sweep of it, it really was kind of beautiful. I came closer to examine it — I wanted to see how he'd gotten them all up there — and then I saw the staples.

PATRICIA.   What?

JONATHAN.   Staples! Tearing through the faces and the bodies. "Look what you've done," I wanted to say, "How could you be so thoughtless? You've ruined everything!" But of

16

course I didn't say that. How could I? He was like a little boy. Beaming. Instead I said, "Dad! What a wonderful job!" *(A beat.)* So, there I was alone in his house, pulling staples out of our family photos. These documents that showed where I came from. Did they *mean* anything to him at all? I mean as artifacts, as proof of a former civilization, when my mother was vibrant and he was young and strong and we were a family? *(A beat.)* That's all gone now, Patty. It's all gone. *(Pause.)*

PATRICIA. You have your wife. *(He nods. Pause.)* She must trust you a lot.

JONATHAN. Why?

PATRICIA. Letting you pop up to see how the old lover made out? Or, ah-ha!, you didn't tell her you were coming!

JONATHAN. No, I told her.

PATRICIA. Too morbid for her taste, huh?, she decided to stay in London?

JONATHAN. No. Actually, she didn't come over.

PATRICIA. Oh?

JONATHAN. She stayed home. Up near New Paltz. We moved out of the city a couple of years ago.

PATRICIA. I know. The article said. I thought it said Vermont.

JONATHAN. No. We bought a farm.

PATRICIA. I know. Some "turn of the century" thing; here we have to ask "turn of *which* century?" So why isn't she here *with* you, your wife? Your big European debut.

JONATHAN. She wanted to. *(A beat.)* She's pregnant.

PATRICIA. *(A beat.)* Ah. Well. A baby. My! Aren't *you* full of news!

JONATHAN. She's pretty far along.

PATRICIA. Congratulations.

JONATHAN. Thanks. I mean, flying was out of the question. Third trimester.

PATRICIA. Of course. So I've heard. Well. Isn't that nice. You'll be a father soon.

JONATHAN. Yeah. Nine weeks or something, yeah.

PATRICIA. Well. This *is* something: Jonathan Waxman a father. Just as you've lost your own.

17

JONATHAN.　Yeah. The irony hasn't escaped me. *(A beat. Going to his wallet.)* Would you like to see a picture?
PATRICIA.　Of the child already?
JONATHAN.　No, of Laura.
PATRICIA.　*(Continuous.)* My God! American technology ...
JONATHAN.　*(Over "technology ...")* I *did* have a sonogram I carried around. It's a boy.
PATRICIA.　A boy.
JONATHAN.　You can tell. You can see his, *you* know, his scrotum.
PATRICIA.　Yes.
JONATHAN.　I meant a picture of Laura. Would you like to ...
PATRICIA.　I've already seen her.
JONATHAN.　How?
PATRICIA.　The article.
JONATHAN.　Oh, right.
PATRICIA.　Remember? Gazing at you like an astronaut's wife?
JONATHAN.　*(Returns the picture to his wallet.)* Oh, well, I thought you might've liked to ...
PATRICIA.　No, I will, show me.
JONATHAN.　It's okay.
PATRICIA.　*Show* me. *(He shows her the photo. A beat.)*
JONATHAN.　That was our wedding.
PATRICIA.　I figured, white dress and everything. How long ago was that?
JONATHAN.　A year ago May. We waited a while. How about you?
PATRICIA.　Me?
JONATHAN.　You and Nick, you've been married *how* long?
PATRICIA.　I don't know, eight or nine years?
JONATHAN.　Eight or nine?, what do you mean?
PATRICIA.　We didn't have much of a wedding. I like her dress. She's so thin. A dancer, right? *(He nods. She returns the photo.)* She seems nice.
JONATHAN.　Yeah, thanks, she is, you'd like her.
PATRICIA.　I'm sure.

JONATHAN. And Nick seems ...
PATRICIA. Don't do that.
JONATHAN. What.
PATRICIA. I tell you I like *your* spouse, you tell me you like *mine*. You don't have to do that.
JONATHAN. I wasn't.
PATRICIA. The fact is ... Nick may seem ... odd ...
JONATHAN. No ...
PATRICIA. *(A small laugh.)* Yes. But he absolutely adores me.
JONATHAN. That's *good*. I'm glad he does. He should. *(A beat. They look at one another.)* And you?
PATRICIA. Look, what do you want?
JONATHAN. What do you mean?
PATRICIA. Do you have some sort of agenda or something?
JONATHAN. No.
PATRICIA. You just happened to be in the neighborhood?
JONATHAN. I wanted to see you again.
PATRICIA. Why?
JONATHAN. I don't know, it felt somehow ... incomplete.
PATRICIA. What did?
JONATHAN. We did. I did. *(A beat.)* I came ... I wanted to apologize.
PATRICIA. *(Smiling.)* Not really.
JONATHAN. What did you think when I called?
PATRICIA. I don't know, I was nonplused. I buried you years ago, then all of a sudden a call from London. You caught me off guard.
JONATHAN. So why did you invite me up?
PATRICIA. You caught me off *guard*, I said. I don't know, what *should* I have done?
JONATHAN. You could've said it was a bad time, you were busy, you had other plans ...
PATRICIA. None of which was true.
JONATHAN. You could've said you had no interest in seeing me again. *(Pause.)* Patty ... *(He makes a conciliatory gesture; She rebuffs him.)*
PATRICIA. I'll give you dinner and a place to spend the night, but, no, Jonathan, I won't forgive you. *(Pause. He goes*

19

for his bag.)
JONATHAN.   Look, maybe this wasn't such a good idea. I should go to a hotel.
PATRICIA.   No! *(A beat.)* Hey, no one here calls me Patty. It's a novelty. *(He drops his bag; She picks up a basket.)* I'm going foraging in my garden for dinner.
JONATHAN.   I'll come with you.
PATRICIA.   You aren't invited. *(A beat.)* You're cold. I think it actually is warmer inside. *(She puts on her jacket and goes. Jonathan soon gravitates toward the painting and looks at it for a while. Nick enters, the depleted bottle of scotch in his hand.)*
NICK.   Oops. *(Jonathan sees him. A beat.)* You've spotted your painting.
JONATHAN.   Yes.
NICK.   I can't tell you how many nights I've stared at the fire and imagined that painting in the flames.
JONATHAN.   Excuse me?
NICK.   Oh, I wouldn't dream of damaging it. It's a work of art. And I am a preservationist by nature. *(A beat.)* It makes Patricia happy to have a piece of you on the wall. Did I say *a piece of you?* I meant a piece *from* you. Or perhaps I *meant* a piece *of* you. A piece of *yours*, at any rate. She gazes at it sometimes, when we're sitting by the fire. It doesn't move me in the same way. No, the eye of the beholder and all that. Drink?
JONATHAN.   No. I painted it a long time ago. When Patty and I were at school. It's strange seeing something I did like twenty years ago and see all these things I couldn't possibly have seen when I painted it.
NICK.   You're rich now, aren't you?
JONATHAN.   What?
NICK.   Patricia tells me you're rich.
JONATHAN.   Oh, God.
NICK.   Read it in some magazine.
JONATHAN.   Well, we talked about that. Actually, I ...
NICK.   *(Over "Actually, I ...")* She said you're rich. You're successful.
JONATHAN.   Those are two different things, really.

NICK. Are they?

JONATHAN. Yes, I think —

NICK. How much do you make in a year?

JONATHAN. Well, I don't —

NICK. Am I out of line?

JONATHAN. Well, maybe.

NICK. How much then?

JONATHAN. It's difficult to say. I've had years in which I've made almost nothing. It's only in the last couple of years —

NICK. *(Over "couple of years —".)* How much would you get for something like that, for instance? *(Meaning the painting on the wall.)*

JONATHAN. A student painting? I have no idea.

NICK. Guess.

JONATHAN. I really don't know.

NICK. Come on. A pivotal work. You said so yourself. A seminal work. How much would a seminal work, given your current currency, if you will, your current notoreity, how much would an old, young Waxman bring?

JONATHAN. I really have no idea.

NICK. Come on, guess.

JONATHAN. In the thousands, certainly. I don't know.

NICK. *(Over "I don't know.")* Oh, I would think more than that.

JONATHAN. Look, I really don't pay much attention to this stuff.

NICK. Don't pay attention to money? Surely you must.

JONATHAN. No, I let my gallery worry about it.

NICK. Art for art's sake, eh? Well, even I, even I who knows, or for that matter, *cares* very little about contemporary values in art, or, even, the value *of* contemporary art, even I would guess you're being awfully stingy on yourself. Considerably more than in the thousands, I would say. More like in the *tens* of thousands, wouldn't you agree?

JONATHAN. Maybe. I really don't know.

NICK. Oh, I would think. A pivotal, precocious painting like this? A seminal masterpiece?

21

JONATHAN.   I don't know. What do you want to hear?
Whatever you want to hear.
NICK.   You.
JONATHAN.   What.
NICK.   I feel as though I've known you all along.
JONATHAN.   Oh, yeah?
NICK.   Your picture. She has this snapshot.
JONATHAN.   What snapshot?
NICK.   A Polaroid. The two of you. Patricia the co-ed. The
party girl. Lithe and sunny. Her tongue in your ear. You,
squirming like a boy caught in a prank. With gums showing.
You don't look at all handsome. She assured me you were. A
costume party of some kind.
JONATHAN.   A costume party?
NICK.   Mm. Patricia in a swimsuit dressed as Miss America.
You're dressed like a jester. A clown. A clown or a pimp.
JONATHAN.   A what?
NICK.   Loud clashing plaids, a camera round your neck.
Sunglasses.
JONATHAN.   Oh. Halloween. I was a tourist.
NICK.   Hm?
JONATHAN.   A tourist. I went dressed as a tourist.
NICK.   A tourist.
JONATHAN.   A visitor, a stranger. An observer. The camera,
the Hawaiian shirt.
NICK.   It doesn't read. (*Jonathan shrugs.*) You look like a
pimp.
JONATHAN.   The idea was a tourist.
NICK.   Hm?
JONATHAN.   Never mind.
NICK.   Patricia had forgotten what you'd dressed up *as*. (*A
beat.*) She thought a pimp.
JONATHAN.   No.
NICK.   Mm. (*A beat.*) What was the idea?
JONATHAN.   The idea?
NICK.   What did it mean? Was there some symbolic value?,
dressing as a tourist?

JONATHAN.   I don't know ...

NICK.   Symbolic of your perception of yourself at that time, perhaps? A transient person? Dislocated?

JONATHAN.   That's interesting. I wonder if —

NICK.   Rubbish. Now, that picture, that photo. Was all I had to go on. For years. Until that New York *Times* article. That one Polaroid she keeps in a box with letters. *(Confidentially.)* I've snooped. There's a postal card from you in that box. One picture postal card. No letters.

JONATHAN.   I didn't write much.

NICK.   Hm?

JONATHAN.   There was no need to write. We were in school together. We saw each other all the time.

NICK.   No, I imagine there *were* letters. Painful collegiate prose. Heartsick poems. Declarations of lust.

JONATHAN.   Sorry.

NICK.   I imagine there *were* letters, but she burned them. Like Hedda Gabler or somebody. Watched with glee while the missives went up in flames.

JONATHAN.   No.

NICK.   I think there *were*. I prefer to think there *were*. And all that remains is an innocuous postal card. From Miami Beach, Florida or someplace.

JONATHAN.   Yes. A visit to my grandparents. Fort Lauderdale.

NICK.   Then there are the stories. Tales of Waxman. The Jonathan Stories. Faraway sounding, exotic. Like from the Old Testament, if you will. Patricia's voice becomes especially animated while telling a Jonathan story. She achieves a new range in a different key. A new tune, a new music entirely. Fascinating. I watch her face. The dimples that sprout! The knowing smiles! Remarkable behavioural findings. *(A beat. He moves his chair closer.)* I've become a Waxmanologist, you see. A Waxmanophile. No, a Waxmanologist. It's my nature. Beneath this reticent exterior lies a probing, tireless investigator. A detective. An historian. And I'm good at my work. I'm compulsive. I'm meticulous. I study the past in order to make sense of the present.

JONATHAN.   I understand.

NICK.   You're smaller in person than I imagined. I held out for a giant. A giant among men. Instead, what's *this*? You're medium-sized. Compact. Razor burn on your neck. Pimple on your cheek. She said you were handsome; you're alright. Perhaps your appeal lies below the belt, but I doubt I'd be surprised.

JONATHAN.   Look, I think I'll — *(Pointing to the door.)*

NICK.   Circumscision isn't common practice in the U.K., you know. *(Jonathan stops.)* Jews still do it the world over, don't they. On religious grounds. Here the risk is too great. Too many accidents. Too many boy sopranos. Here we hold on to our overcoats. *(Patricia returns with her basket filled with vegetables and herbs.)*

PATRICIA.   Oh. Good. You're getting acquainted. *(Jonathan and Nick look at one another.)*

End of Scene

Scene 2

In the black, we hear the din of people chatting in a large room. Lights up: four days later. An art gallery in London. A polished wood floor and a white wall upon which "Jonathan Waxman" is spelled in display letters. It is after Jonathan's opening; plastic cups of wine are scattered about. An attractive, European new-wave-looking young woman (Grete) arranges two Mies van der Rohe-style chairs and sets up a mini tape recorder on a table between them. Jonathan enters.

JONATHAN.   Can we do this quickly?

GRETE.   Yes. Please. Sit down.

JONATHAN.   It's just I promised Antony —

GRETE.   *(While setting up her recorder.)* No, no, sit, let us start immediately.

JONATHAN.   *(Over "immediately.")* There's another reception for me in Hampstead, I really —

GRETE.   *(Over "Hampstead ...")* I am ready. Please. We can begin. *(She gestures for him to sit; he does. She takes a deep breath.)* Now: first may I congratulate you, Mr. Waxman, on such a provocative exhibition.

JONATHAN.   Thank you.

GRETE.   It has been eagerly awaited and does not disappoint.

JONATHAN.   Thank you very much. Can we get to the questions?

GRETE.   Of course.

JONATHAN.   *(Overlap.)* I really don't have time to schmooze, I'm sorry.

GRETE.   You were kind enough to agree to —

JONATHAN.   Well ...

GRETE.   It is a thrill and an honor to finally meet —

JONATHAN.   Thank you. Really, could we please — ?

GRETE.   *(Takes out a stack of index cards.)* Forgive me, I have prepared some questions ... I will begin with the more important ones first.

JONATHAN.   However you want to work it.

GRETE.   *(After a deep breath.)* Mr. Waxman.

JONATHAN.   Yes.

GRETE.   Your depiction of the emptiness and spiritual deadness of middle-class American life in the closing years of the twentieth century have earned you both accolades and admonishment in your own country. Your large, bold canvases of nude men and women who seem as alientated from one another as they they do from their environment have been generating controversy in the art community in the United States for the better part of the last decade. They have also been commmanding huge price tags in the art market. How do you reconcile the success of your work with its rather bleak subject matter?, and, b.) do you think your work speaks as effectively to the rest of the world?, or, like a joke that loses something in translation, is its popularity purely an American phenomenon?

JONATHAN. *(A beat.)* Your English is very good.

GRETE. Thank you. I was a year at N.Y.U.

JONATHAN. Ah. Now: Do I think my work is intrinsically American? Yes. Do I think that it's the equivalent of an inside joke that excludes the rest of the world? Definitely not. Whether the rest of the world *likes* it is another question. I'm not gonna worry too much about it. What was the first part of your question? How do I, what?, reconcile ...

GRETE. The success of your work with its rather bleak subject matter.

JONATHAN. Right. Well, I like to think that people are responding to good art. By good art I mean art that effectively tells the truth, effectively *reflects* the truth, and the truth is often rather bleak, so ... I mean, you're German, right?

GRETE. Yes ...

JONATHAN. Germany's been way ahead of us on this. American art is just starting to get politicized again. Before AIDS, it was all about style and cleverness; we didn't know what to make art *about.* Your country, in Germany, you had guys like Beuys, and Kiefer, making art that terrified and revolted you. *Because they knew what they were making art in response to.*

GRETE. To...?

JONATHAN. To the most horrible event of our time. Yeah, *that* old thing. They were dealing with a society that had literally gone to hell. They were looking for clues among the ashes, looking for answers.

GRETE. Yes, but is it not arguable that events such as America in Vietnam, America in Central America, the failure of the American civil rights movement, to name a few, should have been sufficiently powerful premises for making art during the last generation?

JONATHAN. Yeah, but we're talking about the Holocaust. The horror by which all other horrors are judged.

GRETE.   Horror is horror, is it not? How can you say that one horror is more terrible than another? All societies are guilty of injustice —

JONATHAN.   Whoa. Look, maybe we shouldn't get into this. Let's just talk about the work. Okay? Let's talk about the work.

GRETE.   Very well.

JONATHAN.   Um.... What was I gonna say? Oh, yeah. So anyway, I don't really see my work as bleak. I'm responding to situations that exist in American society that are bleak, maybe, but I'm presenting them in allegorical ways that I hope are provocative and entertaining, even. I mean, I don't set out by saying to myself, "I'm gonna make this really *bleak* painting of an interracial couple trying to make love in a vandalized cemetery." Bleak never comes into it. It's just an image. Just a story.

GRETE.   I'm glad you brought up that painting. *Walpurgisnacht,* no? 1986. A very shocking painting. Some critics have suggested that the couple isn't making love but that the woman is being raped.

JONATHAN.   That's what some critics have said, yes. They've accused me of being racist for showing a black man raping a white woman, but I say it's *their* problem 'cause *they're* the ones who can't fathom a naked black man on top of a naked white woman without calling it rape.

GRETE.   Yes, I've read that explanation before. Some people have suggested that you were being disingenuous in your protestations.

JONATHAN.   Some people would be wrong.

GRETE.   But wouldn't you agree that the title, which means "Witches' Night," could easily mislead?

JONATHAN.   No. If those people were to look beyond their own fears and knee-jerk attitudes toward miscegenation and actually look at the painting, they'd see that the lovers are in a Jewish cemetery that's been desecrated. Stones are toppled, spray-painted with swastikas. That's what the title refers to. I thought I was really hitting people over the head but I guess

27

not. Everyone saw red and failed to see the painting. Just when things quieted down, *feminists* got on my case 'cause the man was on top of the woman!

GRETE.   *(A beat.)* While *Walpurgisnacht* is probably your most famous work — certainly it is your most controversial — and, fittingly, the centerpiece of this exhibition, the talk of the show here today seems to be a painting that to my knowledge has never before been shown.

JONATHAN.   Yes.

GRETE.   A student work. *The Beginning,* it is called.

JONATHAN.   Uh huh.

GRETE.   Painted while you were in your early twenties.

JONATHAN.   Yeah. I only recently came across it again. I'd figured it must've gotten lost or destroyed; student work is *supposed* to get lost or destroyed. But when I found it again, this thing I thought I'd lost, it was like a rush. Every painting I ever did suddenly made sense.

GRETE.   Hm. It is the only painting from your personal collection, I see.

JONATHAN.   Yes.

GRETE.   A very curious painting, Mr. Waxman.

JONATHAN.   Curious how?

GRETE.   On the surface, it appears to be a fairly commonplace, rather youthful study of a seated figure.

JONATHAN.   *(Over "of a seated figure.")* Yeah, but you can't fault the painter for being young. The painting may not be brilliant, but it *is* inspired. I mean, I look at it and I feel the excitement and the, the *danger* of that day all over again.

GRETE.   What was it about that day?

JONATHAN.   I don't know, it was one of those days artists kill for. The kind we always hope we're waking up to, but which rarely comes to pass. I wish I knew what I'd had for breakfast that day or what shirt I was wearing or what I'd dreamed the night before. Burning leaves; I remember the room smelled of burning leaves. Whatever it was, something clicked that day. I was born. My life began. I starting seeing things I'd never seen before.

GRETE. There *is* a kind of ... *openness,* yes?, present in this painting that is virtually absent in your later work. The way the model *engages* the viewer, for instance. Her penetrating, unwavering eye contact. Nowhere else in your work does one find that kind of ... connection.
JONATHAN. *(A beat. She's right.)* Hm.
GRETE. *(Rhetorically.)* I wonder about the model. Who *was* this woman? What role did *she* play? I wonder where she is today?
JONATHAN. *(A beat.)* I have no idea.

End of Scene

Scene 3

The farmhouse. An hour before the start of Scene 1. Patricia is sweeping the floor. Nick watches while preparing tea for the two of them. After a long silence.

PATRICIA. We'll give him our bed. *(He doesn't respond.)* Nick?
NICK. Yes?
PATRICIA. We'll give him our bed. *(A beat.)* Alright?
NICK. Fine. *(Pause.)*
PATRICIA. I'll *offer* it. How's that? I'll *offer* him the bedroom. It'll be up to him. Alright?
NICK. Alright.
PATRICIA. We can sleep on the futon down here. Don't you think? *(Nick shrugs. A beat.)* Don't you think it would be easier?
NICK. Fine.
PATRICIA. *Do* you? Do you think it would be easier?
NICK. *(Over "would be easier?")* Fine. Whatever.
PATRICIA. *Tell* me.
NICK. Yes, I think it would be easier. *(Pause.)*
PATRICIA. God, I should change the sheets. Don't you

29

think?

NICK. Patricia ...

PATRICIA. I really just changed them, should I bother to change them?

NICK. For one night?

PATRICIA. That's what *I* thought: it's only one night. No, I'm not going to change them.

NICK. Don't.

PATRICIA. We can get away with it. He doesn't have to know.

NICK. No.

PATRICIA. They're clean. Tomorrow I'll change them. When he leaves. In the morning.

NICK. Yes. Bright and early. When he leaves. In fifteen hours, eight of which will be spent sleeping. Come have tea. *(Pause. She continues sweeping.)* Patricia, come have your tea.

PATRICIA. Do you mind about the bed?

NICK. What do you mean?

PATRICIA. Do you mind about us giving him the bed?

NICK. Mind?

PATRICIA. I mean, don't you think it would be more comfortable? It's warmer in the bedroom. He'll be cold. Americans are always cold. *(Pause.)* Nick? Do you mind about the bed.

NICK. Have your tea.

PATRICIA. *Do* you? Tell me. *(Pause.)*

NICK. It's only for one night. *(A beat. He reminds her.)* Tea. *(She continues puttering.)* We'll be fine downstairs. We'll light a fire. Warm it up. We've spent nights downstairs in front of the fire before. Right? Haven't we?

PATRICIA. What am I going to do with him?

NICK. What do you *mean* what are you going to do with him? You should have thought about that before.

PATRICIA. *(Over "You should have ...")* I mean it's been fifteen years. What am I going to *do* with him? What do I say?

NICK. Patricia. Really.

PATRICIA. This is foolish. Stupid. Let's go and leave a note.

NICK. Alright, love. Let's.

PATRICIA. "Called away suddenly."

NICK. Yes. Okay. "Dramatic findings in Cotswolds require our presence."

PATRICIA. *(Laughs, then.)* What time is it?

NICK. Nearly half past four.

PATRICIA. Damn. I've got to get to the butcher.

NICK. Have your tea. He's not bloody royalty, you know. *(She puts on her coat.)* Where are you going?

PATRICIA. To get a lamb roast.

NICK. Why don't I come *with* you?

PATRICIA. Someone has to be here.

NICK. You don't expect *me* to ...

PATRICIA. I'll be right back.

NICK. *I* shouldn't be the one who ...

PATRICIA. Please, Nick. Please.

NICK. Wait for him to get here.

PATRICIA. Nick ...

NICK. No, take him with you. Show him the town. He'll be here any time.

PATRICIA. The butcher will be closed.

NICK. *I'll* go to the butcher, you stay.

PATRICIA. You won't know what to get.

NICK. A lamb roast, you said. Let *me* go. You can be here when he arrives. He's *your* friend.

PATRICIA. You're mad about the bed.

NICK. I am not mad about the bloody bed!

PATRICIA. *(Over "the bloody bed.")* If you don't want him to have our bed, *tell* me! *Tell* me you don't want him to! *(Pause.)*

NICK. *(Simply.)* He has it already. *(Pause.)*

PATRICIA. Why didn't you tell me not to invite him?

NICK. Me? Tell you? What do you mean?

PATRICIA. *(Over "What do you mean?")* Why didn't you forbid me from seeing him again?

NICK. Forbid you? How, Patricia? How could I forbid you? *Why* would I? I wouldn't presume to forbid you to do anything.

PATRICIA. *Why? Why* wouldn't you? *(They look at one another. Pause. She starts to exit; He calls.)*
NICK.   Patricia. *(She stops and turns. Pause.)* Come home soon?

End of Scene

Scene 4

15 years earlier. Late afternoon. Spring. Blinds drawn. Jonathan's bedroom in his parents' house in Brooklyn, complete with the artifacts of a lower-middle-class boyhood, the notable exception being a sewing machine. Wearing a vest, suit trousers, and socks, Jonathan is curled up on a bed. His hair is long. There is a tentative knock. Patricia enters. A beat. She whispers:

PATRICIA.   Jonathan? *(She waits, whispers again.)* Jonny? *(She looks around the room, gravitates toward the bookshelf, and begins scanning the titles. After a while, he sits up and sees her looking at a paperback.)* I love your little-boy handwriting. So round. The loopy "J" in "Jonathan," the "o," the "a"s. "This book belongs to Jonathan Waxman." *(Laughs, shows him the book.)* The Man From U.N.C.L.E. I wish I knew you then, Jonny. *(She returns the book to the shelf and continues looking.)*
JONATHAN.   What are you doing?
PATRICIA.   I love looking at people's books.
JONATHAN.   *(Still awaiting a response.)* Patty...?
PATRICIA.   It's like looking into their brain or something. Everything they ever knew. Everything they ever touched. It's like archeology. Lets you into all the secret places.
JONATHAN.   Patty, what are you doing here?
PATRICIA.   Only took me two years to get in the front door. Hey, not bad. — Why isn't *Franny and Zooey* at your place?

JONATHAN.   It is. I have doubles.
PATRICIA.   Oh. *(Pause. They look at one another.)* You look handsome in your suit.
JONATHAN.   *(He begins to put on his shoes.)* Thanks.
PATRICIA.   I don't think I've ever seen you in a suit. Have I? I must have. Did you wear a suit at graduation? No, you wore a cap and gown. What did you wear underneath it? Anything?
JONATHAN.   What time is it?
PATRICIA.   I don't know. *(A beat.)* Your dad kissed me. When I came in? He kissed me. On the lips. He's very sweet, your dad. Said he was glad to see me, he was glad I came. See? He wasn't upset to see me. I told you you were overreacting. He's always kind of had a crush on me I think. *You* know the Waxman men and their shiksas. They're legend.
JONATHAN.   *(Fixing his shirt.)* I should go back down.
PATRICIA.   No. Why? Stay. *(She tries to touch his hair, he moves away. On his rebuff.)* So this is where you and Bobby grew up. *(She sits on a bed.)*
JONATHAN.   That's right ...
PATRICIA.   Funny, it's just how I pictured it. Like one of those Smithsonian recreations? *You* know: those roped-off rooms? "Jonathan Waxman's Bedroom in Brooklyn, Circa 1970." "The desk upon which he toiled over algebra." "The bed in which he had his first wet dream ..."
JONATHAN.   That one, actually.
PATRICIA.   *(She smiles; a beat.)* I loved the oil painting bar mitzvah portraits of you and Bobby over the sofa by the way.
JONATHAN.   What can I tell ya?
PATRICIA.   Oh, they're great. *(A beat; She sees the incongruous sewing machine.)* Sewing machine?
JONATHAN.   She moved it in when I moved out.
PATRICIA.   Ah.
JONATHAN.   The only woman on record to die of empty nest syndrome. *(She goes to him and hugs him.)*
PATRICIA.   Oh, Jonny, I'm sorry ...
JONATHAN.   *(Trying to free himself.)* Yeah. You know, I really

should go back down. My father ... *(They kiss, again and again; he's bothered as her kisses become more fervent. Protesting.)* Patty ... Patricia ... *(She tries to undo his belt.)* Hey! What's the matter with you?

PATRICIA.   Lie down.

JONATHAN.   Patricia, my father is sitting shiva in the living room!

PATRICIA.   Come on, Jonny ...

JONATHAN.   NO, I SAID! Are you crazy?! What the fuck is the matter with you?!

PATRICIA.   You won't let me *do* anything for you.

JONATHAN.   Is this supposed to cheer me up?!

PATRICIA.   I want to *do* something.

JONATHAN.   I don't want sex, Patricia.

PATRICIA.   I've never known anyone who *died* before; tell me what I should do.

JONATHAN.   This isn't *about* you. Do you understand that? This is *my* problem, *my* ... loss, *mine.*

PATRICIA.   But I'm your friend. Aren't I? I'm your lover, for God's sake. Two years, Jonathan ...

JONATHAN.   *(Over "for God's sake ...")* I thought we went *through* this ...

PATRICIA.   I want to be with you. I want to help you.

JONATHAN.   You can't help me, Patty. I'm beyond help.

PATRICIA.   Don't say that.

JONATHAN.   It's true. I am beyond help right now. You can't help me. Your *blow*jobs can't help me.

PATRICIA.   You don't know how I felt not being at the funeral.

JONATHAN.   I'm sorry.

PATRICIA.   No you're not. I was in agony. Really. I couldn't concentrate on anything all day. Knowing what you must've been going through? What kind of person do you think I am? I wanted to be with you so much.

JONATHAN.   So you came over.

PATRICIA.   You didn't say I couldn't. You said the funeral. I came over *after.*

JONATHAN. I meant the whole thing.
PATRICIA. What whole thing?
JONATHAN. The funeral, shiva ...
PATRICIA. You mean I was supposed to keep away from you during all *this?*, like for a *week?* — isn't shiva like a week?
JONATHAN. Patty ...
PATRICIA. Do you know how ridiculous this is? Don't you think you're taking this guilt thing a little too far? I mean, your mother is dead — I'm really really sorry, Jonny, really I am — and, okay, we know she wasn't exactly crazy about me ...
JONATHAN. I'm so burnt out, Patty.... My head is ...
PATRICIA. *(Continuous.)* Not that I ever did anything to *offend* the woman *personally* or anything. I just happened to be born a certain persuasion, a certain incompatible persuasion, even though I'm an atheist and I don't give a damn *what* religion somebody happens to believe in. But did she even bother to get to know me, even a little bit?
JONATHAN. Oh, Patty, this is —
PATRICIA. It's like I was invisible. Do you know how it feels to be invisible?
JONATHAN. What do you think?, my mother's dying wish was keep that shiksa away from my funeral?! Come on, Patty! Grow up! Not everything is about *you.* I know that may be hard for you to believe, but not everything in the world —
PATRICIA. *(Over "in the world —".)* Oh, great.
JONATHAN. *(A beat.)* Let's face it, Patricia, things haven't exactly been good between us for months.
PATRICIA. What do you mean? Your mother's been *sick* for months. How can you make a statement like that?
JONATHAN. What, this is a surprise to you what I'm saying?
PATRICIA. Hasn't your mother been dying for months.
JONATHAN. I don't really have the strength for this right now.
PATRICIA. Hasn't she? So how can you judge how things have been between us? Her dying has been weighing over us, over both of us, for so long, it's colored so much ...

JONATHAN.   *(Over "it's colored so much ...")* Look ... if you *must* know —
PATRICIA.   What.
JONATHAN.   If you *must* know ... *(A beat.) I* was the one who didn't want you there. It wasn't out of respect to my mother or my father or my grandmother, it was me. I didn't want to see you. I didn't want you there, Patty. I didn't want to have to hold *your* hand and comfort *you* because of how cruel my mother was to you, I didn't want that ... I didn't want to have to deal with your display of —
PATRICIA.   Dis*play?*
JONATHAN.   Your display of love for me. Your concern. It was all about *you* whenever I thought about how it would be if you were with me! I didn't want you there, Patty. I'm sorry. *(A beat.)* I guess when something catastrophic like this happens.... You get to thinking.
PATRICIA.   Yes? Well? *(Pause.)*
JONATHAN.   I don't love you, Patty. *(He smiles lamely and reaches for her as if to soothe her as she goes to get her bag. She groans, punches his arm, and goes. He stands alone for a long time before moving slowly over to the sewing machine. He clutches a pillow and gently rocks himself. As he begins to cry: lights fade to black.)*

END OF ACT ONE

ACT TWO

Scene 5

Lights up: The farmhouse. A few hours after the end of Scene 1. Patricia and Jonathan are seated at the table after dinner. The wine is nearly finished; they are all somewhat disinhibited. Nick is standing nearby, looking through the exhibition catalogue.

JONATHAN.   Drive down with me tomorrow.

PATRICIA.   I don't *go* to London, I try to *avoid* London.

JONATHAN.   *(Over "... avoid London.")* You can take the train back Tuesday night, after the opening.

PATRICIA.   *(Over "after the opening ...")* The crowds, tourists, everything so bloody expensive.

JONATHAN.   Don't worry about money; everything is on me.

PATRICIA.   Why should everything be on you?; I don't want everything to be on you.

JONATHAN.   *(Over "I don't want everything ...")* What, you think I'd invite you down and make you pay for it?

PATRICIA.   God, Jonathan ...

JONATHAN.   Let me treat you to a couple of days in London!

PATRICIA.   You sound like such an American!

JONATHAN.   Come on, we'll hang out for a couple of days, it'll be fun.

PATRICIA.   What are you talking about?

JONATHAN.   We'll do the museums, you'll come to the opening, I'll introduce you to people ...

PATRICIA.   I don't need to meet people, I know enough people.

JONATHAN.   *(Over "... enough people.")* I mean artists. Writers, actors. You wouldn't believe the people coming.

PATRICIA.   Uh huh.

37

JONATHAN. Hey, I'll take you to Caprice.

PATRICIA. Is that a restaurant?

JONATHAN. *Yes*, it's a restaurant.

PATRICIA. I *told* you, your name-droppings are wasted on me.

JONATHAN. Patty, let me do this. I want you to be my *guests, both* of you.

PATRICIA. Well, I don't know about Nick; he *completely* falls apart in London, don't you, Nick.

NICK. Hm?

PATRICIA. *(Continuing, to Jonathan.)* That's never any fun, holding his hand as we brave the crush on the pavement. Besides, he couldn't get away.

JONATHAN. Then *you* come.

PATRICIA. No. I couldn't. What are you saying? I don't like big cities anymore either, they get me nervous. I don't even remember the last time I was there.

JONATHAN. Then you're due for a visit. It's really changed, London. Even in the five or six years since I was last over.

PATRICIA. You were here? Five or six years ago?

JONATHAN. Yeah, just a ... quick thing, *you* know. Passing through.

PATRICIA. Uh huh. *(A beat.)* I know: must have been a year ago Christmas. Whenever my mother comes, she drags me to every bit of crap on the West End; Lloyd Webber's latest ditty. Do you know what they get for that slop?

JONATHAN. Patty.

PATRICIA. I can't just take off and go; some of us have to *work* for a living, you know.

JONATHAN. Oh, well! Excuse *me*!

PATRICIA. *(Over "Excuse me!")* I have data to collect. I have responsibilities, people who count on me; I can't just come and go as I please.

JONATHAN. I'm not asking you to quit your job and run away with me. Two or three days!

PATRICIA. Two or *three*? A minute ago it was a couple.

JONATHAN. Patty ...

PATRICIA. I can't get away. This is a very exciting time for us. Has Nick told you about the project?

JONATHAN. A Roman latrine?

PATRICIA. Is that all he told you? Nick! *Tell* Jonathan.

NICK. What.

PATRICIA. About the project. *(To Jonathan.)* He loves to minimize. *(Jonathan nods. To Nick.)* Tell him what you found.

NICK. Patricia ...

PATRICIA. Oh, you! *(To Jonathan.)* He's impossibly modest. Nick found, not only the latrine, but a late medieval rubbish pit.

JONATHAN. A garbage dump?

PATRICIA. Yes!

NICK. *I* didn't find it, Patricia, we *all* found it ...

PATRICIA. Do you have any idea what a valuable find that is, medieval rubbish? Seriously. Shoes, rags, broken plates. It was one of those happy accidents and Nick led us to it.

NICK. I *didn't.* I wish you wouldn't ...

PATRICIA. Everything you need to know about a culture is in its rubbish, really. What they wore, what they ate. It's a treasure trove. Tons of it. I sift through parcels of ancient rubbish every day, analyze it, catalog it. That's what I do. Every day. Now you know. I shouldn't have told you.

JONATHAN. Why not?

PATRICIA. Sounds fascinating.

JONATHAN. No, it does. *(She gives him a look. He laughs.)* It does. — Come to my opening.

PATRICIA. Stop it.

NICK. Um ... *(They look at him. A beat. Referring to the catalogue:)* I'm looking at your paintings ...

JONATHAN. Yes...?

NICK. And, honestly ... I don't get it.

JONATHAN. What don't you get?

NICK. I don't get ... what's all the fuss about?

JONATHAN. What fuss?

PATRICIA. Oh, Nick. Be nice.

NICK. I mean, is this all it takes to set the art world ablaze?

PATRICIA. Nick's idea of art is the *Mona Lisa.*

NICK. My idea of art, in point of fact, Patricia, begins and ends with the Renaissance. Everything before it was ceremonial, arts-and-crafts — hardly "art," really; everything since, well, everything since has been utter rubbish.

JONATHAN.   Are you kidding? How can you say that? *(To Patricia.)* All of modern art, he's dismissing just like that?

NICK.   *(Over "just like that?")* But it's all been done, hasn't it. The so-called modern age, as far as I can tell, has been one long, elaborate exercise, albeit a futile one, to reinvent what had already been perfected by a handful of Italians centuries ago.

JONATHAN.   But the world is constantly reinventing *itself*. How can you say that Leonardo's world view expresses *our* world, or Picasso's even?

NICK.   Picasso. Now *there* was an energetic little bloke.

JONATHAN.   Am I supposed to shrink in the shadow of the great masters and pack it all in? Say the hell with it, why bother?

NICK.   If you had any sense? Yes. *(Patricia giggles naughtily.)* Absolutely. Why bother, indeed? *(To Patricia.)* How is it that all the artists I've ever known feel that what they do is so vital to society? *(She laughs some more.)* Does it ever occur to them that if they were wiped off the face of the earth the planet would survive intact?

JONATHAN.   *(To Patricia.)* Gee, you didn't tell me you'd married such an art lover.

NICK.   Art was devised as a celebration of beauty, was it not? I mean, does *this* celebrate beauty? *(Waving the catalogue.)* This, this ... pornography?

PATRICIA.   Nick!

JONATHAN.   *(Smiling, to Patricia.)* That's okay.

NICK.   *(Over "That's okay.")* Because as far as I can tell that's precisely what this is. And not very *good* pornography at that.

JONATHAN.   Really. Well.

PATRICIA.   Nick was raised by a puritanical mother.

NICK.   *Fuck* that, Patricia. I look at this ... "art" and I see pornography. Tell me what's there that eludes me.

JONATHAN.   I'm not gonna *tell* you what to see. If you see pornography ...

40

NICK. I don't *get* it, is what I'm saying. If I don't get it, is it my failure or yours? Enlighten me. Help me see.

JONATHAN. You know, you usually don't have the luxury of painters whispering in your ear when you're looking at their paintings, telling you what to see. That's not the job of the artist. The job of the artist is not to spell everything out. *You* have to participate.

NICK. Participate.

JONATHAN. Yes. You play an active role in all this; it's not just me, it's not just the artist.

NICK. Alright ... what's this, then? *(Flips the catalogue to a particular painting.)*

JONATHAN. You can't judge the work like *that*, black-and-white reproductions in a catalogue ...

NICK. *(Over "... in a catalogue...")* What is this if not pornography?

JONATHAN. Come on, Nick, use your head a little. What do you see?

NICK. You actually want me to tell you?

JONATHAN. Yeah. Describe to me what you see.

NICK. Alright. I see what *appears* to be a painting ...

JONATHAN. Oh, man ...

NICK. *(Continuous.)* executed with minimal skill in terms of knowledge of basic anatomy ...

JONATHAN. You really have to see the *paint*ing ...

NICK. *(Continuous.)* of what *appears* to be a couple of mixed race fornicating in what *appears* to be a cemetery, is it?

JONATHAN. Don't be so literal! Yes, that's what it appears to be on the surface, but what's it really saying?

PATRICIA. Let me see. *(Nick shows it to her.)*

JONATHAN. *(Continuous.)* What's going on there? It's an allegory, it's telling a story. Use your imagination!

PATRICIA. The woman is being raped.

JONATHAN. Ah ha. Is she?

PATRICIA. Well, yes, look at her hands. They're fists.

NICK. They aren't necessarily fists; they're just poorly drawn hands.

JONATHAN. Jesus.

41

NICK.   That's what I mean by the apparent disregard for basic traditions in art like knowing the skeletal structure of the human hand.

JONATHAN.   But you know what hands look like.

NICK.   What?! Is that your response?: I *know* what hands...?

JONATHAN.   What I'm saying is, it's not my job to photographically recreate the skeletal structure of the human hand.

NICK.   What *is* your job? You keep talking about what isn't your job; what *is* your job? Is it your job to paint well, or not?

JONATHAN.   What do you mean by "paint well?" You obviously have very limited ideas about painting. I'm telling you, if you guys came down to London, I'll take you around, we'll look at art, I could *show* you ...

NICK.   If one were to *buy* one of these ... paintings — presuming, of course, one could afford to — where would one put it?

JONATHAN.   What?

NICK.   I mean, they're quite large, aren't they.

JONATHAN.   Fairly.

NICK.   One would have to have quite a large wall on which to hang such a painting and, preferrably, an even larger room in which to view it properly. (Art *is* meant to be seen, no?) And that room would undoubtedly have to sit in an even more capacious house. Not your standard taxpayer, I take it.

JONATHAN.   No.

NICK.   Say *I* wanted to buy one of these.

JONATHAN.   You? One of those?

NICK.   Mm. What would I do?

JONATHAN.   Well, for starters, you couldn't; they're already sold.

NICK.   *All* of them?

PATRICIA.   *(Leafing through the catalogue; sotto.)* "Saatchi Collection," "Union Carbide Collection," "Mobil Corporation Collection ..."

JONATHAN.   All of the existing ones, yes.

NICK.   The "existing" ones?

JONATHAN.   Yes. And there's a waiting list for the paintings I have yet to paint.

PATRICIA. A waiting list? You're joking.

JONATHAN. No.

NICK. You mean there are people on Park Avenue or in Tokyo, who have walls in their living rooms especially reserved for the latest Waxman, Number 238?

JONATHAN. Yeah.

NICK. It doesn't matter which painting, as long as they get their Waxman?

JONATHAN. It's not like this is new, you know; artists have always lived off of commissions.

NICK. So, wait, these art lovers, these poor, unsuspecting — rather, *rich*, unsuspecting — patrons of the arts have bought, sight unseen, a painting you have not yet painted?

JONATHAN. Yes.

PATRICIA. Amazing, Jonny. Pre-sold art.

NICK. What happens if they don't like it?

JONATHAN. What?

NICK. The painting. Say it doesn't please them. The colors clash with the carpet; the image makes madam blush. What then? Are they entitled to a refund? Can they hold out for the next one off the line?

JONATHAN. If they really dislike it, I guess, but it hasn't happened.

NICK. So how many can you expect to do in a year?

JONATHAN. One every five or six weeks? Figure ten a year.

NICK. Ten a year. At roughly a quarter million dollars per painting ...

JONATHAN. (*Over "per painting..."*) Now, wait a minute. What is this fascination with my finances? Ever since I got here you've been hocking me ...

NICK. (*Over "Ever since I got here ..."*) Patricia, are you aware of how fortunate we are to be the proud owners of our own, actual, *already painted* painting by Jonathan Waxman? And a seminal Waxman at that!

JONATHAN. Look, why should I have to *apologize* for my success?

PATRICIA. Nobody's asking you to.

JONATHAN. (*Continuous.*) What am I supposed to do? Re-

43

ject the money? Lower my price? What would *that* accomplish? Would it make me a better artist if I were hungry again?

NICK. I don't know. Would it?

PATRICIA. *(A beat; looking at the catalogue.)* They *do* look like fists, Jonathan.

JONATHAN. What if they are fists? What difference does it make?

PATRICIA. It makes a very big difference. It changes everything. If they're fists, then that suggests that she's being taken against her will. If they're not.... Is the painting about a black man raping a white woman, or is it about a couple screwing in a cemetery?

JONATHAN. Oh. You're saying it's ambiguous.

PATRICIA. I'm saying it's confusing. You can't have intended both things.

JONATHAN. Why not? I've got you thinking about it haven't I?

NICK. But thinking about what? What does it *mean*? If *you* can't say, unequivocally ...

PATRICIA. *(To Jonathan.)* He has a point. It's all about shock, then. Effect. You can't *mean*, "What difference does it make," Jonathan, that just isn't good enough.

JONATHAN. *(Over "... isn't good enough.")* You know I don't entirely mean that. I mean, *my* intention is irrelevant; it's all about what you make of it.

NICK. Either way you look at it, it has about as much impact as a smutty photo in a porno mag.

JONATHAN. You can't get past the flesh, can you.

NICK. What?

JONATHAN. This is very interesting. All you see is the flesh. Of course! You surround yourself with *bones* all day. I mean, here you are, freezing your asses off ...

PATRICIA. Jonathan ...

JONATHAN. *(Continuous.)* cataloguing bones whose flesh rotted away centuries ago. No wonder my paintings scare you!

NICK. Scare me, did you say?

JONATHAN. Yes. They're ... voluptuous, dangerous. They deal with unspeakable things, fleshy things. *That's* what's going

44

on in my paintings. The lengths people go to, living people go to, in order to feel something. Now. Today. *(Pause.)*

PATRICIA.   We thought we'd put you in our bedroom.

JONATHAN.   What?

PATRICIA.   We thought we'd put you ...

JONATHAN.   In *your* room? No, you don't have to do that.

PATRICIA.   No bother.

JONATHAN.   Where are *you* gonna sleep?

PATRICIA.   Down here.

JONATHAN.   No no, I'll sleep down here.

PATRICIA.   The bedroom is actually warmer.

JONATHAN.   I don't mind.

NICK.   Are you sure?

JONATHAN.   Yeah.

PATRICIA.   No, trust me, the bedroom, it's really no problem.

NICK.   *(Over "no problem.")* Patricia, he said he doesn't mind.

JONATHAN.   I don't.

NICK.   See? *(To Jonathan.)* Yes, why *don't* you stay downstairs?

JONATHAN.   Fine.

PATRICIA.   But the electric *blank*et is upstairs. He's going to need the electric blanket.

JONATHAN.   *(Over "electric blanket.")* Don't worry about me.

NICK.   I'll bring it down.

PATRICIA.   The mattress-warmer, actually. It's under the sheet. You'll have to strip the bed. It really would be easier ...

NICK.   *(Over "easier ...")* So I'll strip the bed. The bed needs stripping anyway.

PATRICIA.   *(A beat; to Nick.)* Are you sure?

NICK.   Yes. I'll take care of it. Leave it to me.

JONATHAN.   Thank you. *(Nick goes. Pause.)* I hope I'm not ...

PATRICIA.   You hope you're not what?

JONATHAN.   I don't know, it seems that my being here ...

PATRICIA.   Yes?

JONATHAN.   *You* know.... Things seem a little, I don't know ... prickly, maybe? I mean with Nick?

PATRICIA.   I haven't seen this much life in him in years.

JONATHAN. Really. *(Pause.)*
PATRICIA. I married Nick to stay in England.
JONATHAN. *(A beat.)* Oh.
PATRICIA. They would've deported me. After my degree.
JONATHAN. Ah.
PATRICIA. My visa, *you* know, it was a student visa. It expired. I couldn't go home. How could I go home? Back to my broken-down mother? I couldn't. My skeptical father, who humored me through all my crazy pursuits? I had no one to go home to. No, this made sense. I found that I could survive here. I had to stay.
JONATHAN. *(A beat.)* Does he know?
PATRICIA. I'm sure he does. You mean why...? *(Jonathan nods.)* I'm sure he knows. It was certainly no secret. He knew I needed a way to stay.
JONATHAN. I don't understand you. How can you be so cool about this?
PATRICIA. What?
JONATHAN. The man is obviously crazy about you; he's like a blushing *school*boy around you ...
PATRICIA. I know.
JONATHAN. How can you do this? I never thought you'd be *capable* of something like this. You were such a passionate girl, Patty ...
PATRICIA. Oh, God, spare me ...
JONATHAN. You were the "student of the world!" Remember? No, really, how do you ... I mean, passion, sex, love.... You just decided, what, you don't need those things anymore?, you just shut that part of you all out?
PATRICIA. Yes. Exactly. My "passion" nearly did me in, now, didn't it.
JONATHAN. Oh, come on, don't lay this on me. That's bullshit. You call yourself an expatriate? You're no expatriate, you're just hiding!
PATRICIA. Who the hell are *you* to judge — ?!
JONATHAN. Why do you live with him?
PATRICIA. Why? He's my husband.
JONATHAN. That's not a reason. Why do you live with him

if you don't love him?
PATRICIA.   Who said I don't love him?
JONATHAN.   You just said yourself, you married Nick ...
PATRICIA.   *This is the best I can do! (Pause.)*
JONATHAN.   Don't say that. It isn't even true. I know you too well.
PATRICIA.   *Knew* me. You *knew* me. You don't *know* who I am. *(A beat. Nick appears with a bundle of bedding. They look at him. Pause.)*
NICK.   Um.... Shall I.... Would you like me to make your bed?

End of Scene

Scene 6

The gallery in London. This scene is the continuation of Scene 2.

GRETE.   You just said your definition of good art is "art which effectively reflects the truth." Do you think it is your responsibility as an artist to always tell the truth?
JONATHAN.   In my work? Yes.
GRETE.   And in your personal life?
JONATHAN.   My personal life is my personal life. Look, if my work tells the truth, then I think people are compelled, they *have to* deal with it, they can't not. I like to shake 'em up a little, I admit it. People see my stuff at a gallery, a museum, and the work *competes* for their attention. They're preoccupied, overstimulated. All I can hope is maybe — *maybe* — one night, one of my images'll find its way into their unconscious and color their dreams. Who knows? Maybe it'll change their perception of something forever. I mean, in art, as in life, we tend to affect people in ways we can't always see. You can't possibly know what that other person has taken away with her. *(A beat.)* You can't see it. And just 'cause you can't

see it doesn't mean it didn't happen.

GRETE. Hm. Getting back to "good art ..."

JONATHAN. Okay, let me ask you something: When *we* talk about good art, what are we talking about? Stuff we like? Stuff our friends make? We're talking about value judgments. Most people, do you think most people, most Americans — my *father* — do you think most people have any idea what makes good art?

GRETE. Hm.

JONATHAN. The little old lady who paints flowers and pussycats at the YMCA — and *dazzles* her friends, I'm sure — I mean, does that little old lady make good art? I mean, why not?, her cat looks just *like* that. I'm not putting her down; I think it's great she's got a hobby. But is what she does good art? See, most people ... I remember, years ago, the big van Gogh show at the Met?, in New York? The place was packed. Like Yankee Stadium. Buses emptied out from all over; Jersey, Westchester. All kinds of people. The masses. Average middle-class people. Like they were coming into the city for a matinee and lunch at Mamma Leone's. Only this was Art. Art with a capital A had come to the shopping mall generation and Vincent was the chosen icon. Now, I have nothing against van Gogh. Better him than people lining up to see the kids with the big eyes. But as I braved that exhibit — and it was rough going, believe me — I couldn't help but think of Kirk Douglas. Kirk Douglas should've gotten a cut of the house. See, there's this Hollywood packaging of the artist that gets me. The packaging of the mystique. Poor, tragic Vincent: he cut off his ear 'cause he was so misunderstood but still he painted all these pretty pictures. So ten bodies deep they lined up in front of the paintings. More out of solidarity for Vincent (or Kirk) than out of any kind of love or passion for "good art." Hell, some art lovers were in such a hurry to get to the postcards and prints and souvenir placemats, they strode past the paintings and skipped the show entirely! Who can blame them? You couldn't *experience* the paintings anyway, not like that. You couldn't *see* *any*thing. The art was just a backdrop for the *real* show that was happening. In the gift shop!

GRETE. Hm.

JONATHAN. Now, you got to admit there's something really strange about all this, this kind of *frenzy* for art. I mean, what *is* this thing called art? What's it for? Why have people historically drunk themselves to death over the creation of it, or been thrown in jail, or whatever? I mean, how does it serve the masses? *Can* it serve the — I ask myself these questions all the time. Every painting I do is another attempt to come up with some answers. The people who crowded the Met to look at sunflowers, I mean, why *did* they? 'Cause they *thought* they should. 'Cause they thought they were somehow enriching their lives. Why? *'Cause the media told them so!*

GRETE. You seem to have such contempt ...

JONATHAN. Not contempt; you're confusing criticism with contempt.

GRETE. *(Continuous.)* for the very same people and the very same system that has made you what you are today.

JONATHAN. What I am today? What *am* I today? I just got here. People like *you* suddenly care what I have to say.

GRETE. I *do* care.

JONATHAN. I know you do. It cracks me up that you do; it amuses me. You know, up till like eight or nine years ago, let's not forget, I was painting a*part*ments for a living. Apartments. Walls. Rooms. I was good at it, too. I'd lose myself all day while I painted moldings, then I'd go home and do my *own* painting all night. A good, simple, hard-working life. Then, like I said, like nine years ago, my world started getting bigger. I couldn't even retrace the steps; I can't remember how it happened. All I know is I met certain people and got a gallery and a show and the public started to discover my work. The night of my first opening, it's like these strangers witnessed a birth, like the work had no life before they laid eyes on it. We know that's ridiculous, of course, but this is what happens when you take your art out of your little room and present it to the public: it's not yours anymore, it's *theirs*, theirs to see with their own eyes. And, for each person who sees your work for the first time, you're discovered all over again. That begins to take its toll. You can't be everybody's discovery. That gets to be very demanding. Who *are* these people who are suddenly throwing money at you and telling you how wonderful and talented you are? What do *they* know? You begin to believe them. They begin to want things from you. They begin to expect things. The work loses its importance; the importance is on "Waxman."

GRETE.   Would you prefer to have remained an outsider?

JONATHAN.   Preferred? No. It's cold and lonely on the outside.

GRETE.   And yet being cozy on the inside ...

JONATHAN.   "Cozy?"

GRETE.   *(Continuous.)* seems to make you uncomfortable as well. Is this not an illustration of that Jewish joke?

JONATHAN.   What Jewish joke?

GRETE.   Forgive my paraphrase: Not wanting to be a member of a club that would also have you as a member?

JONATHAN.   That's not a Jewish joke, that's Groucho Marx.

GRETE.   Groucho Marx, then. Is he not Jewish?

JONATHAN.   Yeah, so?

GRETE.   Well, does not that joke apply to the problem Jews face in the twentieth century?

JONATHAN.   What problem is that?

GRETE.   The problem of being on the inside while choosing to see themselves as outsiders ...

JONATHAN.   Is that a Jewish problem?

GRETE.   *(Continuous.)* even when they are very much on the inside?

JONATHAN.   "Very much on the inside"? What is this?

GRETE.   *(Over "What is this?")* Perhaps I am not expressing myself well.

JONATHAN.   No, I think you're probably expressing yourself *very* well.

GRETE.   All I am suggesting, Mr. Waxman, is that the artist, like the Jew, prefers to see himself as alien from the mainstream culture. For the Jewish *artist* to acknowledge that the *contrary* is true, that he is *not* alien, but rather, *assimilated* into that mainstream culture —

JONATHAN.   *(Over "mainstream culture —".)* Wait a minute

wait a minute. What is this *Jewish* stuff creeping in here?

GRETE.   You are a Jew, are you not?

JONATHAN.   I don't see what that —

GRETE.   *(Over "what that —".) Are* you?

JONATHAN.   Yeah; so?

GRETE.   I am interested in the relationship between the artist and the Jew, as Jonathan Waxman sees it.

JONATHAN.   Who *cares* how Jonathan Waxman sees it? I'm an *American* painter. *American* is the adjective, not *Jewish, American.*

GRETE.   Yes, but your work calls attention to it.

JONATHAN.   How?

GRETE.   The Jewish cemetery in *Walpurgisnacht, —*

JONATHAN.   *One* painting.

GRETE.   One *important* painting — the depictions of middle class life, obviously Jewish —

JONATHAN.   How can you say that? "Obviously" Jewish.

GRETE.   I have studied your paintings, I have done research on your upbringing ...

JONATHAN.   Oh, yeah?

GRETE.   *(Continuous.)* I have written many critical studies for art journals in my country. The middle-class life you explore — It is safe to say that your paintings are autobiographical, are they not?

JONATHAN.   In what sense? Of course they're autobiographical in the sense that they come from *me,* they spring from *my* imagination, but to say that the subjects of my paintings are *Jewish* subjects, because a Jew happened to paint them, that's totally absurd.

GRETE.   Mr. Waxman, I cannot tell to what you have most taken offense: the suggestion that was made, or that it was made by a German.

JONATHAN.   *(A beat.)* Look, maybe we should ...

GRETE.   Please, just one more question ...

JONATHAN.   Can we please move on? Let's move on.

GRETE.   Of course. *(A beat.)* Mr. Waxman, you speak with charming self-effacement about your much-celebrated career. You say you are amused by your sudden fame ...

JONATHAN.   Yes.

GRETE.   *(Continuous.)* and seem to view it as an unwanted but not unwelcome bonus, that making good art is all you have ever wanted to do.

JONATHAN.   Yes.

GRETE.   And yet — forgive me, Mr. Waxman — I am confused. If, as you claim, you had no interest in celebrity, why would you hire a public relations firm?

JONATHAN.   This is how you change the subject?

GRETE.   There have been whispers, Mr. Waxman. *(She says "vispers.")* Why would you hire a publicist if —

JONATHAN.   You think I'm the only painter who has a publicist? This is the reality. You reach a certain point in your career, an *artist* reaches a certain point, where he achieves a certain amount of recognition —

GRETE.   Yes, I know, you said. I do not question that.

JONATHAN.   Will you let me finish please? If you're gonna make a statement like that ...

GRETE.   I am sorry.

JONATHAN.   *(Continuous.)* then at least let me make my point.

GRETE.   Please.

JONATHAN.   An artist who's achieved a certain amount of celebrity, very quickly, there are suddenly all these demands being placed on him. I've talked about that.

GRETE.   Yes.

JONATHAN.   People want you. Interviews, parties, schools. The problem becomes *time.* Where do you find the time to work?, to do the thing that made you famous? This is where having a publicist comes in. The publicist helps manage your social obligations. And if the painter doesn't have one, the gallery does, so what's the big deal?

GRETE.   No, no, I understand. Perhaps I did not phrase my question correctly.

JONATHAN.   Cut the crap, Miss; your English is impeccable.

GRETE.   Mr. Waxman, the whispers I have heard ...

JONATHAN.   Again with the "vispers!"

GRETE.   Is it true that you hired a public relations firm *two years before* your first success,

JONATHAN. Oh, come on. What is this, the Inquisition? Art is a business, you know that.

GRETE. Two years *before*, to promote your standing in the art community —

JONATHAN. My "standing" — ?

GRETE. *(Continuous.)* More importantly, in the art-buying community.

JONATHAN. What are you saying?, I bought my career? I bought my reputation?, what?

GRETE. Mr. Waxman ...

JONATHAN. *(Continuous.)* What about the work? Why aren't we talking about the work? Why must it always come down to business? Huh? *I'm* not doing it, and yet you accuse *me* ...

GRETE. *(Over "... and yet you accuse me.")* Is it true or is it *not* true?

JONATHAN. That's irrelevant. True or not true, who cares?

GRETE. *(Over "... who cares?")* It *is* relevant.

JONATHAN. How? How?

GRETE. It is relevant if you espouse to be a visionary of truth.

JONATHAN. *(Over "... visionary of truth.")* I espouse nothing! What do I espouse? I paint pictures! You're the one who comes up with these fancy labels, people like *you!*

GRETE. *(Over "people like you!")* How can you talk about truth? Mr. Waxman, how can you talk about truth when your own sense of morality —

JONATHAN. What do *you* know about morality?

GRETE. *(Continuous.)* When your own sense of morality is so compromised and so —

JONATHAN. Huh? What do *you* know with your sneaky little Jew-baiting comments.

GRETE. I beg your pardon.

JONATHAN. Don't give me this innocence shit. You know exactly what I'm talking about.

GRETE. *(Over "what I'm talking about.")* No, I am sorry, I have no idea.

JONATHAN. You think I haven't picked up on it? Huh?

You think I don't know what this is all about?
GRETE.   Mr. Waxman, this is all in your imagination.
JONATHAN.   My imagination?! I'm imagining this?! I'm
imagining you've been attacking me from the word go?
GRETE.   Mr. Waxman!
JONATHAN.   You have, Miss, don't deny it. You expect me
to sit here another minute? What do you take me for? Huh?
What the fuck do you take me for? *(He abruptly goes.)*
GRETE.   Mr. Waxman ... *(Pause. She presses a button on the
tape recorder. We hear the tape rewind.)*

End of Scene

Scene 7

*The farmhouse. A few hours after the end of Scene 5. The
middle of the night. Jonathan, bags packed, his coat on,
tears a sheet of paper out of his sketchbook, turns off the tea
kettle before its whistle fully sounds and prepares a cup of
tea. The painting, wrapped in newspaper, leans against the
kitchen table. He takes six 50-pound notes out of his wallet
and leaves them under the honey pot on the kitchen table.
Nick has quietly come downstairs and lingers in the darkness. He emerges from the shadows. Jonathan is startled
when he sees him and spills his tea.*

JONATHAN.   Oh. Shit. Hi.
NICK.   Sorry.
JONATHAN.   I didn't see you.
NICK.   My fault. *(A beat.)* Are you alright?
JONATHAN.   A little wet; I'm alright.
NICK.   *(A beat.)* Couldn't sleep.
JONATHAN.   No.
NICK.   I mean *I* couldn't.
JONATHAN.   Oh. Me, neither.
NICK.   Was the futon...?

JONATHAN. No, it's fine. Did the kettle — ? I'm sorry if the whistle ...

NICK. No. *(A beat.)* Shall I get the fire going again?

JONATHAN. No, you don't have to do that, I could've done that. No, I think I'll just head back early.

NICK. Oh. I see.

JONATHAN. Yeah, I think I'll, *you* know ...

NICK. Back to London.

JONATHAN. Yeah.

NICK. Hm. *(A beat.)* You won't even wait until breakfast?

JONATHAN. No, I'd better not.

NICK. Patricia will be disappointed.

JONATHAN. Yeah, I'm sorry about that.

NICK. She had planned something, I think. Breakfast.

JONATHAN. Oh, that's too bad.

NICK. *(A beat.)* So you won't get to see the dig.

JONATHAN. I guess not.

NICK. I was going to take you.

JONATHAN. Next time.

NICK. Yes. Next time.

JONATHAN. *(A beat.)* It's just, I've got so much to do when I get back.

NICK. *(Nods; a beat.)* Did I...? Was I...? I mean I hope I wasn't too ... *(A beat.)* You weren't ... sneaking out, were you?

JONATHAN. Sneaking — ? No. No, I just thought I'd get an early start.

NICK. It's half past three. You'll be in London before seven. That's quite an early start you're getting.

JONATHAN. I couldn't sleep. I thought I might as well hit the road.

NICK. I see. Well. Patricia will be so disappointed. *(A beat.)* You weren't sneaking out on Patricia.

JONATHAN. No. Of course not. I was gonna leave her a note.

NICK. I'll give it to her.

JONATHAN. I haven't written it yet.

NICK. Oh.

JONATHAN. I was just gonna sit down and write it.

NICK. Please. Carry on. *(Jonathan sits. Pause.)* What were you going to say?

JONATHAN. Hm?

NICK. In this note. What were you going to *say?*

JONATHAN. I'm not sure.

NICK. What were you going to tell her? That would be difficult. Finding the right words. Patricia will be *so* disappointed. She was so looking forward to breakfast. I don't know what she'll do. I might have to comfort her. *(A beat.)* She doesn't sleep with me, you know.

JONATHAN. Oh.

NICK. Not that I was ever her type. There was a certain challenge to be found in that. I thought she would *never*, not with me. She was so ... *attractive*, you know, so confident, so American. The first time she slept with me I thought it must have been because I was her supervisor. I'm sure that was why. When it happened a second time, well, I didn't know *what* to think; I chose to think there was hope. Yes, I opted for hope. In a moment of uncharacteristic brazenness, I asked her to marry me. She accepted. I don't know why. I have my suspicions. *(A beat.)* From time to time, I'll fortify myself with stout and kiss her neck, feel her tit, lay with my head there.

JONATHAN. Nick.

NICK. Sometimes she'll let me. She'll even stroke my hair. Once she kissed my head. I wanted to reach up and kiss her mouth, but why get greedy and piss her off?

JONATHAN. Why don't you go back to bed?

NICK. Some nights she'd respond — oh, she'd respond, or initiate even — and I would rush into it foolishly, trying not to feel I was somehow being rewarded. I take what I can get; I'm English. *(A beat.)* She succumbed to my charms tonight, though. Tonight she acquiesced. Did you hear us? *(Jonathan shakes his head; he's lying.)* Oh. What a shame. It was brilliant. *(A beat. He sees the money.)* What's this?

JONATHAN. What.

NICK. Under the honey pot. Money is it? A gratuity? Leaving a gratuity?

JONATHAN. No. Just a little cash.

NICK. A little cash? This is 300 pounds. Why are you leaving 300 pounds?

JONATHAN. I thought ...

NICK. What.

JONATHAN. I thought it could be useful.

NICK. Useful? Of course it could be useful. Money is always useful. Why are you leaving 300 pounds?

JONATHAN. I thought I could help you out.

NICK. Me?

JONATHAN. You and Patricia.

NICK. With 300 pounds?

JONATHAN. Yeah. I happened to have a lot of cash on me, I thought I ...

NICK. (Over "I thought I ...") You thought you could help us out, unload some cash ...

JONATHAN. You know what I mean.

NICK. (Continuous.) lend us a hand, by leaving 300 pounds.

JONATHAN. I wanted to say thank you.

NICK. *Thank* you?! *Thank* you?!

JONATHAN. (Over "... you?!") Don't be offended.

NICK. Who's offended? Who even *suggested* offense had been taken?

JONATHAN. I thought maybe.... You sounded ...

NICK. Do you wish for me to be offended?

JONATHAN. Oh, please. Look, can we —

NICK. Do you *wish* for me —

JONATHAN. No. I'm sorry; you're taking it the wrong way.

NICK. Am I? You leave 300 pounds under my honey pot ...

JONATHAN. Nick. Jesus. I can't win with you, can I. Please. Just accept my thanks.

NICK. Your thanks for what?

JONATHAN. For letting me spend the night.

NICK. 300 pounds? For "letting" you? 300 pounds for letting you spend the night? If I'd known there was a price, I'd have charged you considerably more than 300 pounds. Considering the damages to my home and happiness. Yes, like German reparations after the war. I should thank *you*. Your proximity served as a welcome marital aide. Interesting going at it like

57

that. Each for his or her own reasons, yet mutually satisfying just the same. It *is* kind of like war, isn't it.

JONATHAN.   I never meant you any harm.

NICK.   Never meant me...?

JONATHAN.   You act as if I'm to blame for your unhappiness. I'm sorry if you're unhappy. I never meant you any harm. We only met this afternoon ...

NICK.   Have I spoiled the surprise?

JONATHAN.   What surprise?

NICK.   Were we to awaken to find you gone but 300 pounds in your stead, under the honey pot? Economic aid, is that it? Jonathan Waxman: Our American Cousin. Our Jewish uncle.

JONATHAN.   Enough with the "Jewish," Nick.

NICK.   You're right; cheap shot. A Robin Hood for our time, then. Stealing from the rich and giving to the poor. Hey, not entirely off the mark, is it?, stealing from the rich and giving to the — You are quite the charlatan it turns out.

JONATHAN.   Am I?

NICK.   Oh, yes. You shit on canvas and dazzle the rich. They oo and ah and shower you with coins, lay gifts at your feet. The world has gone insane. It's the emperor's new clothes.

JONATHAN.   *(Reaching for it.)* Look, if you don't want my money ...

NICK.   Uh uh uh. Don't get me wrong: I will take your money. Gladly. *And* insult you. I will bite your hand. With relish. Your money is dirty, Wax Man. Hell, I don't care; I could use a few quid. *(Patricia, awakened from a deep sleep, enters wearing a robe.)*

PATRICIA.   What is happening?

NICK.   Our guest is leaving. Getting an early start. He left a gratuity.

PATRICIA.   What?

NICK.   *(Shows her the money.)* 300 quid.

JONATHAN.   Look, I thought it would be best for everyone if I was gone in the morning.

PATRICIA.   Is that what you thought? Why? Was the evening so unbearable?

JONATHAN.   No ...

PATRICIA. I thought it went pretty well, considering.

JONATHAN. *(Over "considering.")* It did.

PATRICIA. It could have been excrutiating.

JONATHAN. I know; it could've been. I was gonna write you a note.

PATRICIA. A note. You know, Jonathan?, you have this incredible knack for dismissing me whenever I've finished serving whatever purpose you've had in mind for me. Just incredible.

JONATHAN. Patty.... Look: it was really good to see you.

PATRICIA. What kind of shit is that?: "good to see you." I'm not one of your fucking patrons. *(Nick slips out of the room.)*

JONATHAN. Alright, already! What do you want me to say? Did you think it was easy, calling you and coming up here like this?

PATRICIA. Nobody asked you to!

JONATHAN. I had to! Okay? I had to see you again; I had to face you.

PATRICIA. This is how you face me? By sneaking out? *(She sees the painting. A beat.)* What are you doing with *that?* Oh, no you don't. Absolutely not.

JONATHAN. I'm only talking about a loan.

PATRICIA. Why?

JONATHAN. For the show.

PATRICIA. But it's my painting.

JONATHAN. I know.

PATRICIA. You gave it to me.

JONATHAN. I know I did. I'd like you to *loan* it to me. For the show. My gallery'll send you all the legal ...

PATRICIA. *(Over "... all the legal ...")* What the hell do you want with this painting? It isn't even that good.

JONATHAN. I don't care how good it is. It's missing something, the show. *I'm* missing something. I've been looking for a link, a touchstone. When I saw this painting ...

PATRICIA. It's *me* in that painting, Jonathan. You gave it to *me.*

JONATHAN. Don't worry about privacy, the loan can be

59

anonymous ...

PATRICIA.   I sat for that painting. The day we met. You gave me that painting.

JONATHAN.   *(Over "You gave me that painting.")* It'll be anonymous, nobody has to know your name.

PATRICIA.   That's not the point. I don't want my painting hanging in a gallery!

JONATHAN.   It's only for five weeks. In five weeks, they'll ship it back to you.

PATRICIA.   It doesn't mean anything to anyone else; it means something to me. I don't understand — Is *this* why you came?

JONATHAN.   What? No.

PATRICIA.   *(Continuous.)* Hoping I'd provide the missing link?

JONATHAN.   I wanted to *see* you. I had no idea you'd even have it. As far as I knew you'd hacked it to bits fifteen years ago.

PATRICIA.   Why didn't I?

JONATHAN.   You tell me.

PATRICIA.   So, what was your plan, you were just going to pack it up and go?

JONATHAN.   I was going to write you a letter. To explain.

PATRICIA.   What, that you were stealing it?

JONATHAN.   Borrowing it.

PATRICIA.   Taking it. Without my knowledge. That's stealing! You were stealing my painting!

JONATHAN.   I didn't think it would matter so much to you. I thought you'd be, I don't know, flattered.

PATRICIA.   Flattered?!

JONATHAN.   To be in the show.

PATRICIA.   God, Jonathan, the arrogance! So you just take what you want now, hm? Is that what fame entitles you to? I don't understand what's happened to you, Jonathan, what's happened to your conscience? You had a conscience, I know you did. Guilt did wonders for you. It made you appealing. Now I don't *know*. You've lost your *good*ness or something. Your spirit. *(Nick has slipped back in.)*

JONATHAN.   You're right; I have. I *have* lost something. I've

lost my way somehow, I don't know.... I've been trying to retrace my steps.... Ever since my father died ... I'm nobody's
son anymore, Patty. They're all gone now, all the
disappointable people. There's no one left to shock with my
paintings anymore. When I saw this painting, though, it was
like all of a sudden I remembered where I came from!
There's a kind of purity to it, you know?, before all the
bullshit. Patty, I just need to hold onto it.
NICK. How much is it worth to you?
JONATHAN. What?
NICK. *(Gets the painting.)* Start the bidding. What's it worth?
PATRICIA. Nick. For God's sake ...
JONATHAN. I'm only talking about borrowing it.
NICK. Borrowing is no longer an option. Either you buy it
outright ...
JONATHAN. You're not serious.
PATRICIA. Nick! This is none of your business!
NICK. None of my — ? It most certainly *is* my business.
PATRICIA. It isn't yours to sell!
NICK. Oh, let him have the bloody painting and let's be on
with it?
PATRICIA. No!
NICK. Please, love. Let him take it out of our home. At
long last, please.
PATRICIA. It isn't for sale!
NICK. *Let* him, Patricia. Let him take it to London.
PATRICIA. No, Nick!
NICK. Let him buy it. Doesn't it make sense, love? Think
of it: This one painting ...
PATRICIA. No!
NICK. We'll make some money, love. Tens of thousands.
PATRICIA. This painting doesn't have a price!
NICK. It's our future, love! Our future was sitting on the
wall all along. Think of it: We can *save* some money, we can
pay our debts. We can get on with it. *(Pause. Softly.)* Let him
take the painting, love. *(Nick and Patricia look at one another for
a long time. She lets him take the painting; he gives it to Jonathan.)*
There you go.

JONATHAN. *(To Patricia, who is facing away.)* You're sure this is what you want?

NICK. Yes. Absolutely. Send us a check. Pounds or dollars, either is acceptable. As long as it's an obscene amount.

JONATHAN. It will be.

NICK. Good. *(A beat.)* Goodbye, Jonathan.

JONATHAN. Goodbye.

NICK. *(To Patricia.)* I think I'll ... go back to bed. *(He starts to go. She takes his hand.)*

PATRICIA. Soon. *(Nick leaves. Long pause.)* I can't describe the pleasure I had being your muse. The days and nights I sat for you. It thrilled me, watching you paint me. The connection. The connection was electric. I could see the sparks. I never felt so alive as when I sat naked for you, utterly still, obedient. I would have done anything for you, do you know that?

JONATHAN. Patty ...

PATRICIA. Isn't that shameful? A girl so devoid of self? I would have done anything. *(A beat.)* You know, even after that last time in Brooklyn, I never actually believed that I'd never see you again.

JONATHAN. No?

PATRICIA. No, I always held out the *possibility.* But *this* time ... *(A beat.)* We won't be seeing each other again. Will we. *(A beat. He shakes his head. A beat.)* Hm. I wonder what that will be like. *(They continue looking at one another as lights fade.)*

End of Scene

Scene 8

About 17 years earlier. A painting studio at an art school. Easels in motley array. We can see the model dressing behind a screen. A class has just ended; all who remains is a youthful, shaggier Jonathan, who continues to paint. Soon, the model, the young Patricia, enters and finishes dressing in silence. Finally:

PATRICIA. How's it going?
JONATHAN. Hm?
PATRICIA. How's it —
JONATHAN. Oh. Fine. *(Pause.)*
PATRICIA. You want me to shut up?
JONATHAN. What? No.
PATRICIA. Can I see?
JONATHAN. Uh ...
PATRICIA. Please? I won't —
JONATHAN. It's.... It's really not there yet.
PATRICIA. Oh, come on ...
JONATHAN. You'll get the wrong idea.
PATRICIA. I won't say anything.
JONATHAN. I don't know, I'm still ...
PATRICIA. Not a peep.
JONATHAN. *(A beat.)* Alright. *(She goes to the easel, stands beside him for a long time trying not to show her reaction.)* I'm playing around with the point of view. See how the —
PATRICIA. Shhh ... *(She takes a long beat, then walks away, resumes dressing. Pause.)*
JONATHAN. Well...?
PATRICIA. What. *(He looks at her expectantly.)* You told me not to say anything.
JONATHAN. You can say *something* ...
PATRICIA. I'm going on a diet effective immediately.
JONATHAN. I knew you'd take it the wrong way. It's purposely distorted. I'm trying something. You see how it looks like I'm looking *down* at you and *at* you at the same time? That's why the figure, your figure, looks a little ...
PATRICIA. Huge. No, I'm kidding, it's good. Really. It's me. I have this mental image of myself ... I think I'm a Botticelli, but I always come out Reubens. *(A beat.)* You're very good, you know.
JONATHAN. I am?
PATRICIA. Oh, come on, you know it. I looked around during the break. You're the best in the class.

JONATHAN. Nah, I'm just having a good day.

PATRICIA. You want me to shut up so you — ?

JONATHAN. That girl Susan's the best I think.

PATRICIA. She is not. Are you kidding?

JONATHAN. She's very slick, I know, but her color ...

PATRICIA. I'm Patricia, by the way.

JONATHAN. I know.

PATRICIA. I mean, we haven't been formally introduced; you've been staring at my *bush* all *day* but we haven't ...

JONATHAN. I'm Jonathan.

PATRICIA. I know. *(They shake hands. Pause.)*

JONATHAN. You're a good model.

PATRICIA. Yeah? This is my first time ever.

JONATHAN. Is it really? I wouldn't have known.

PATRICIA. You mean it?

JONATHAN. Yeah. I really wouldn't have known. You're good.

PATRICIA. What makes a model good?

JONATHAN. I don't know. You're very steady.

PATRICIA. Steady.

JONATHAN. *You* know, you keep the pose.

PATRICIA. Oh.

JONATHAN. *You* know what I mean.

PATRICIA. So that's all it takes? Steadiness?

JONATHAN. No. I don't know, I mean, when you're working from a model ...

PATRICIA. Yeah...?

JONATHAN. *(Continuous.)* you kinda have to distance yourself.

PATRICIA. Uh huh.

JONATHAN. I mean, just because one of you is naked, it's not necessarily a sexual thing.

PATRICIA. It's not?

JONATHAN. No. It's.... You have to maintain a certain objectivity, a certain distance. See, it's the whole *gestalt*.

PATRICIA. The *gestalt*.

JONATHAN. Yeah. It's the room and the pose and the canvas. It's the *moment*. The light, the way you look ...

PATRICIA. You like the way I look?

JONATHAN. *(A beat.)* Yes.

PATRICIA. *(A beat.)* I can't believe I actually signed up to do this (my mother would *die*). It isn't hard, all I have to do is sit still and let my mind wander. I do that all the time anyway. Why shouldn't I get paid for it? I was watching them burn leaves out the window. The fire was beautiful. — Hey, you want me to get undressed?

JONATHAN. What?

PATRICIA. So you can work.

JONATHAN. No you don't have to do that ...,

PATRICIA I don't mind ...

JONATHAN. Your time is up; you don't get paid overtime.

PATRICIA. I don't care.

JONATHAN. No, really, I can paint from memory. Really.

PATRICIA. Why should you paint from memory? I'm *here* ... I mean, I *do* have my film history class ...

JONATHAN. Is that your major? Film?

PATRICIA. No, I have no major. I'm a dilettante.

JONATHAN. Oh.

PATRICIA. You want to know what I'm taking this semester? I'm taking American Film Comedy from Chaplin to Capra, Women in Faulkner's South, Poetry Workshop (talk about dilettantes), Introduction to Archeology. And, you know what? It's wonderful, I am having such a wonderful time. I never thought being a dilettante could be so rewarding. I'm interested in a lot of different things so why should I tie myself down with a major, you know?

JONATHAN. *(Humoring her.)* Uh huh.

PATRICIA. You're humoring me.

JONATHAN. *(Lying.)* No.

PATRICIA. My *father* always humors me; you're humoring me.

JONATHAN. I'm not.

PATRICIA. What's wrong with someone admitting she's a dilettante?

65

JONATHAN. Nothing.

PATRICIA. All it means is that I see myself as a student of the world. A student of the world. I'm young, I have time. I want to try a *lot* of things. Is that something to be ashamed of?

JONATHAN. No. It's just.... I've never been able to do that. I mean, all I ever wanted to do was paint. I wanted to be an artist, ever since I was a little kid. I was like four and I could copy amazing. I don't know, if I could just paint all the time, maybe once in a while go out for Chinese food ... that's all I want out of life. *(Pause.)*

PATRICIA. You know?, you do this *thing* ...

JONATHAN. What.

PATRICIA. *(A beat.)* I've been watching you. While you work?

JONATHAN. You've been *watch*ing me?

PATRICIA. Uh huh. There's this *thing* you do I've noticed. With your mouth.

JONATHAN. What do I do with my mouth?

PATRICIA. When you're painting.

JONATHAN. What do I *do*?!

PATRICIA. *(A beat.)* You sort of stick your tongue out.

JONATHAN. Oh. So you're saying I look like an idiot?

PATRICIA. *(Laughing.)* No, it's ... I'm sorry.... It's *cute* ...

JONATHAN. Oh, great ...

PATRICIA. It *is*. I mean, your concentration ... *(A beat.)* It's sexy.

JONATHAN. Oh, I'm sure. This dribbling down my ... a real turn-on.

PATRICIA. *(Laughing.)* It is ... *(She suddenly kisses his mouth.)*

JONATHAN. *(Surprised, he recoils.)* Hey!

PATRICIA. Sorry. I'm sorry.... Look, why don't you just paint ... *(Quickly gathers her things.)*

JONATHAN. No, wait ... I didn't mean "Hey!" I meant "Oh!" It came *out* "Hey!"

PATRICIA. Are you gay or something?

JONATHAN. No.... Surprised. I'm not used to having girls ...

PATRICIA. What.

JONATHAN. I don't know. Come on so strong.

PATRICIA. Sorry. It won't happen again. *(She goes.)*

JONATHAN. Oh, great ...

PATRICIA. *(Returning.)* Let me ask you something: If I hadn't kissed you, would you have kissed me?

JONATHAN. No.

PATRICIA. What *is* it with you?! We're staring at each other all day..., I'm *naked*, totally exposed to you ... your tongue is driving me insane — the attraction is mutual, wouldn't you say? I mean, wouldn't you say that?

JONATHAN. Yeah ...

PATRICIA. Then what is it? *(Pause.)*

JONATHAN. You ... scare me a little.

PATRICIA. I scare you.

JONATHAN. You do. You scare me.... A lot, actually ...

PATRICIA. How could I scare you? I'm the scaredest person in the world.

JONATHAN. Oh, boy ... *(Takes a deep breath; a beat.)* You scare me ... 'cause of what you represent. I know that sounds ...

PATRICIA. *(Over "I know that sounds ...")* For what I r — What do I represent? Dilettantism? Nudity? Film studies?

JONATHAN. *(A beat.)* You aren't Jewish. *(He smiles, shrugs. A beat.)*

PATRICIA. You're kidding. And all these years I thought I was.

JONATHAN. Look, this is hard for me. It's a major thing, you know, where I come from ...

PATRICIA. What, your mother?

JONATHAN. Not just my mother. It's the six million! It's, it's the diaspora, it's the history of the Jewish people! You have no idea, the *weight.* You got to remember I come from Brooklyn. People where I come from, they don't like to travel very far, let alone intermarry. They've still got this ghetto mentality: safety in numbers and stay put, no matter what. It's always, "How'm I gonna get there?" *(She smiles.)* No, really.

"How'm I gonna get there?" and "How'm I gonna get home?" "It'll be late, it'll be dark, it'll get cold, I'll get sick, why bother? I'm staying home." This is the attitude about the world I grew up with. It's a miracle I ever left the house! *(She laughs. They look at one another for a long beat.)*

PATRICIA.   So now what do we do?

JONATHAN.   What do you mean?

PATRICIA.   This is it? No discussion? The end?

JONATHAN.   I *told* you. I'm sorry. I can't ... get *involved* with you.

PATRICIA.   "Involved"? What does that *mean*, "involved"? You can't *look* at me?, you can't *talk* to me? What are you so afraid of?

JONATHAN.   I don't even know.

PATRICIA.   We're talking about a *kiss*, Jonathan, a kiss, some coffee, and maybe spending the night together.

JONATHAN.   Uy.

PATRICIA.   We are not talking about the future of the Jewish race.

JONATHAN.   See, but I think we are.

PATRICIA.   My God, they've got you brainwashed! Is this what they teach you in Hebrew school?

JONATHAN.   This is how it starts, though, Patricia: a kiss.

PATRICIA.   You make it sound like a disease!

JONATHAN.   Well, maybe it is. Maybe it's wrong and destructive and goes against the natural order of things. I don't know. Maybe it just shouldn't be.

PATRICIA.   And maybe it's the greatest adventure!

JONATHAN.   Assimilation as Adventure. Sounds like one of your courses.

PATRICIA.   *Don't humor me!* It's very condescending, Jonathan, it really is.

JONATHAN.   *(Over "it really is.")* I'm sorry I'm sorry.

PATRICIA.   I come from a tribe, too, you know. Maybe not one with the same history as yours, but still.... You're as exotic to me as I am to you! You're an artist! An artist has to experience the world! How can you experience the world if you

say "no" to things you shouldn't have to say "no" to?!
JONATHAN.   *(A beat. He smiles.)* Do me a favor?, get my
mother on the phone? *(He gestures to the easel with his brush,
meaning: "I should get back to work." A beat. She kicks off her
shoes. Quietly.)* No, no, don't, really.... What are you doing?
PATRICIA.   Don't paint from memory. *I'm* here, Jonathan.
(A beat.) Paint *me. (They're looking at one another. As she slowly
unbuttons her blouse, and he approaches, lights fade to black.)*

END OF PLAY

RANDOM NOTES
ON *SIGHT UNSEEN*

HOW THE PLAY WAS DEVELOPED

In 1988 South Coast Repertory commissioned a new work from me which began life as a play called *Heartbreaker*. In it, over the course of nine unchronological scenes, a nice Jewish boy named Jonathan Waxman examined moments from various intimate relationships in his life, beginning with his erotic awakening at the age of 12 and ending just as he is about to become a father. After reams of rewrites and workshops at Sundance and at South Coast, it became clear to me that the play wasn't working, that it wasn't likely to work the way I had hoped and, more important, that I was losing interest in it. So I shelved *Heartbreaker*. A few months later I looked at it with fresh eyes and found a new angle on the material. I retained the protagonist's name but instead of his being a fledgling artist I made him one who was fabulously successful — a crucial decision which ended up galvanizing the play and opening exciting new areas for exploration. I also held onto the germ of three of *Heartbreaker's* stronger scenes — those depicting aspects of Jonathan's relationship with Patricia: their meeting, their break-up, and their reunion several years later. Those three scenes, substantially rewritten, formed the arc, and five entirely new scenes were created (including those in which Jonathan is interviewed by the German art critic).

In January 1991 the totally reconceived *Sight Unseen* (as it was now called after months of being known as "The England Play") was given a reading at New Dramatists with Kate Nelligan, Peter Friedman, Anthony Heald and Wendy Makkena. That draft was somewhat beefier than the current version but the cubistic structure was virtually the same as it is now. The play was further cut and read again in March, this time at South Coast, where it had its world premiere six months later. The play was even leaner by the time it opened in January 1992 at Manhattan Theatre Club.

THINGS TO BE CONSIDERED
WHEN STAGING THIS PLAY

SCENE TRANSITIONS

I had always imagined that a turntable be used to help move the show along and director Michael Bloom and the show's designers, Cliff Faulkner at South Coast and, later, Jim Youmans at MTC, came up with an ingenious rotating system by which the various settings were concealed and revealed. I urge future productions to try something similarly effective.

In the first conversation I had with Michael about *Sight Unseen,* I expressed my concern that the play move as swiftly as possible from scene to scene and that the stage never be plunged into darkness as people stumbled around moving furniture. In Michael's deft staging of the scene transitions we always see at least one of the actors in character on stage. As the lights shift at the end of Scene 1, for instance, Grete appears as if preparing for the interview she will conduct with Jonathan in the following scene; before you know it, the turntable has revolved, the other actors have made their exits, and she is able to step directly into the art gallery setting.

THE BEGINNING OF THE PLAY

Michael Bloom cleverly devised a brief, silent prologue in which Jonathan appears on stage while the set for the final scene is in place along with elements from the first scene. Jonathan enters as if he is entering a memory play of his own creation, fingers the bristles of a paint brush and sets the play in motion; literally, the turntable revolves to the farmhouse kitchen setting of Scene 1, thereby establishing the conceit of the play within perhaps the first 30 seconds. Directors of future productions may want to play around with similar ideas, or maybe not.

THE CHARACTER OF NICK

Nick should not be played like an oaf or a fool who suddenly shows great verbal dexterity. He is, as Patricia observes, somewhat "odd," but in the manner of a hermetic academic who is most comfortable with inanimate artifacts. He is nearly paralyzed with shyness in unfamiliar social situations, such as when he greets his wife's charismatic former lover. He is not an alcoholic but a man for whom alcohol provides welcome disinhibition in the fraught situation at hand; it lubricates his tongue.

THE FLASHBACK SCENES

In the two scenes in which we see Jonathan and Patricia in their early twenties, the actors should not *play* young, rather capture the *essence* of their characters' youthful personas. In other words, these scenes must not be played as cartoonish representations of post-adolescent behavior. Nor should they be overly concerned with period flavor to connote the past.

THE INTERVIEW SCENES

Like my caveat about the flashback scenes, the scenes with Grete should not be played facilely, like a comedy sketch in which a caricatured Germanic inquisitor skewers Jonathan. It is absolutely essential that these scenes be subtle and ambiguous, with our perception shifting from one beat to the next.

A few clues: 1) Grete is truly thrilled, almost to the point of obsequiousness, to be meeting the subject of her research in the flesh. 2) There should definitely be a sexual undercurrent to the point-counterpoint. 3) In Jonathan's speech at the beginning of the second interview scene, it's no accident that he says, "you can't possibly know what that person has taken away with *her* [emphasis added]." He's talking about Patricia. Remember that, in real time, these scenes take place *after* his visit to Patricia and Nick.

ALTERNATE DIALOGUE

If the actor portraying Jonathan is larger than "medium-sized," the following should replace Nick's speech on p. 24:

NICK. You're less imposing in person than I imagined. I held out for a god. A god among men. Instead, what's *this?* You're mortal. Razor burn on your neck. Pimple on your cheek. She said you were handsome; you're alright. Perhaps your appeal lies below the belt but I doubt I'd be surprised.

MUSIC

Michael Roth composed a gorgeous, elegiac, jazzy theme for the South Coast Rep premiere that Michael Bloom and I liked so much that we decided to use it again for the play's New York production. The tape is available through Dramatists Play Service; you might want to consider using it in your production as well.

Donald Margulies
July, 1992

PROPERTY LIST

Bag (JONATHAN) with:
    2 wine bottles
    art show catalogue
Hard roll (NICK)
Scotch bottle (half full) (NICK)
Scotch glass (NICK)
Tea cup with tea bag
String bag (PATRICIA) with:
    4 potatoes
    3 canned goods
    carrots
    package of veal
Purse (PATRICIA) with:
    glasses
    shoes
Gallery wine cup
2 tea cups
Wine bottle, open (half full)
Greens for basket
Glass of water
Keys (PATRICIA, JONATHAN)
3 wine glasses
3 napkins
2 saucers
Cookie box with cookies
2 bowls with spoons
Gallery chairs
Gallery table
Pillow
Blanket
Shiva plate and glass
Broom
Dustpan
Glass (NICK)

Wallet with money (JONATHAN)
Purse (GRETA) with:
    tape player
    note cards
    steno pad
    pen
    folder
Sketchbook (JONATHAN)
Pen (JONATHAN)
Paint pallet and brush
Pallet knife
Tube of paint
Paint rag
Wrapped painting (JONATHAN)
Water in Hudson (under sink)
Tool basket (on floor)
Candlestick (counter)
Potato bowl (counter)
Kettle (counter)
Cutting board
2 knives
Cork screw
Tea pot and cozy (sink top)
4 tea cups (cabinet)
Tea tin (cabinet)
Trash can (under sink)
Metal bowl (under sink)
Towel (top of drawers)
Towel (dishrack)
Dishrack
3 utensils (bottom drawer, wrapped in napkins)
Scotch bottle, almost full (in small cabinet)
Easel
Crate
Table
2 chairs
Breadcrumbs (on table)

Honey pot (on table)
Silver can
Trick brush
Books (in bedroom panel)
Pillows (in bedroom panel)

COSTUME PLOT

ACT ONE

Scene 1

PATRICIA
Brown sweater
Green corduroy pants
White, long-sleeve t-shirt
Suede boots
White socks
Barrette
Green plaid overcoat

JONATHAN
Black jeans
Black no-buck oxfords
Grey print socks
Grey/green silk shirt
Black belt
Tweed jacket
Tweed overcoat
White/black silk scarf
Watch

NICK
Thermal T-shirt
Grey corduroy pants
Suspenders
Plaid shirt
Blue sweater
Thermal socks
Work boots
Down vest
Watch

Scene 2

GRETE
Black zipper coat
Black miniskirt
Black tights
Black suede buckle shoes
Black headband
Jewelry (brooch, bracelet, necklace, earrings)

JONATHAN
Maroon jacket
Maroon/green tie
Black jeans
Grey/green silk shirt
Black no-buck oxfords
Grey print socks
Watch

Scene 3

PATRICIA
same as Scene 1, starting without overcoat; add during scene

NICK
same as Scene 1

Scene 4

PATRICIA
Blue floral dress
Blue shawl
White sandals
Grey purse

JONATHAN
Grey, 3-piece suit
Blue/white pinstripe shirt
Blue tie
Black oxfords
Black socks
Yarmulke
Mourning pin
Eye glasses

ACT TWO

Scene 5

PATRICIA
Same as Scene 1, without overcoat

JONATHAN
Same as Scene 1, without overcoat

NICK
Same as Scene 1, without down vest

Scene 6

GRETE
Same as Scene 2

JONATHAN
Same as Scene 2

Scene 7

PATRICIA
Brown plaid robe

JONATHAN
Same as Scene 1

NICK
Thermal T-shirt
Grey corduroy pants
Suspenders (down)

Scene 8

PATRICIA
Floral wrap skirt
Salmon top
Brown sandals

JONATHAN
Navy t-shirt
Army fatigues
Red bandana
Sneakers
Eye glasses

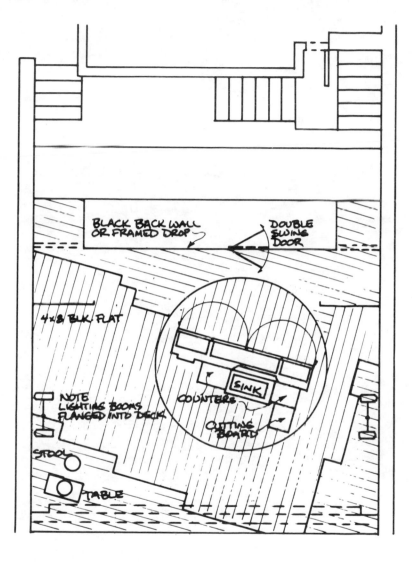

SCENE DESIGN
"SIGHT UNSEEN"
(DESIGNED BY JAMES YOUMANS FOR MANHATTAN THEATRE CLUB)

NEW PLAYS

★ **MONTHS ON END by Craig Pospisil.** In comic scenes, one for each month of the year, we follow the intertwined worlds of a circle of friends and family whose lives are poised between happiness and heartbreak. "…a triumph…these twelve vignettes all form crucial pieces in the eternal puzzle known as human relationships, an area in which the playwright displays an assured knowledge that spans deep sorrow to unbounded happiness." *—Ann Arbor News.* "…rings with emotional truth, humor…[an] endearing contemplation on love…entertaining and satisfying." *—Oakland Press.* [5M, 5W] ISBN: 0-8222-1892-5

★ **GOOD THING by Jessica Goldberg.** Brings us into the households of John and Nancy Roy, forty-something high-school guidance counselors whose marriage has been increasingly on the rocks and Dean and Mary, recent graduates struggling to make their way in life. "…a blend of gritty social drama, poetic humor and unsubtle existential contemplation…" *—Variety.* [3M, 3W] ISBN: 0-8222-1869-0

★ **THE DEAD EYE BOY by Angus MacLachlan.** Having fallen in love at their Narcotics Anonymous meeting, Billy and Shirley-Diane are striving to overcome the past together. But their relationship is complicated by the presence of Sorin, Shirley-Diane's fourteen-year-old son, a damaged reminder of her dark past. "…a grim, insightful portrait of an unmoored family…" *—NY Times.* "MacLachlan's play isn't for the squeamish, but then, tragic stories delivered at such an unrelenting fever pitch rarely are." *—Variety.* [1M, 1W, 1 boy] ISBN: 0-8222-1844-5

★ **[SIC] by Melissa James Gibson.** In adjacent apartments three young, ambitious neighbors come together to discuss, flirt, argue, share their dreams and plan their futures with unequal degrees of deep hopefulness and abject despair. "A work…concerned with the sound and power of language…" *—NY Times.* "…a wonderfully original take on urban friendship and the comedy of manners—a *Design for Living* for our times…" *—NY Observer.* [3M, 2W] ISBN: 0-8222-1872-0

★ **LOOKING FOR NORMAL by Jane Anderson.** Roy and Irma's twenty-five-year marriage is thrown into turmoil when Roy confesses that he is actually a woman trapped in a man's body, forcing the couple to wrestle with the meaning of their marriage and the delicate dynamics of family. "Jane Anderson's bittersweet transgender domestic comedy-drama …is thoughtful and touching and full of wit and wisdom. A real audience pleaser." *—Hollywood Reporter.* [5M, 4W] ISBN: 0-8222-1857-7

★ **ENDPAPERS by Thomas McCormack.** The regal Joshua Maynard, the old and ailing head of a mid-sized, family-owned book-publishing house in New York City, must name a successor. One faction in the house backs a smart, "pragmatic" manager, the other faction a smart, "sensitive" editor and both factions fear what the other's man could do to this house— and to them. "If Kaufman and Hart had undertaken a comedy about the publishing business, they might have written *Endpapers*…a breathlessly fast, funny, and thoughtful comedy …keeps you amused, guessing, and often surprised…profound in its empathy for the paradoxes of human nature." *—NY Magazine.* [7M, 4W] ISBN: 0-8222-1908-5

★ **THE PAVILION by Craig Wright.** By turns poetic and comic, romantic and philosophical, this play asks old lovers to face the consequences of difficult choices made long ago. "The script's greatest strength lies in the genuineness of its feeling." *—Houston Chronicle.* "Wright's perceptive, gently witty writing makes this familiar situation fresh and thoroughly involving." *—Philadelphia Inquirer.* [2M, 1W (flexible casting)] ISBN: 0-8222-1898-4

DRAMATISTS PLAY SERVICE, INC.
440 Park Avenue South, New York, NY 10016 212-683-8960 Fax 212-213-1539
postmaster@dramatists.com www.dramatists.com

NEW PLAYS

★ **BE AGGRESSIVE by Annie Weisman.** Vista Del Sol is paradise, sandy beaches, avocado-lined streets. But for seventeen-year-old cheerleader Laura, everything changes when her mother is killed in a car crash, and she embarks on a journey to the Spirit Institute of the South where she can learn "cheer" with Bible belt intensity. "...filled with lingual gymnastics...stylized rapid-fire dialogue..." –*Variety*. "...a new, exciting, and unique voice in the American theatre..." –*BackStage West*. [1M, 4W, extras] ISBN: 0-8222-1894-1

★ **FOUR by Christopher Shinn.** Four people struggle desperately to connect in this quiet, sophisticated, moving drama. "...smart, broken-hearted...Mr. Shinn has a precocious and forgiving sense of how power shifts in the game of sexual pursuit...He promises to be a playwright to reckon with..," –*NY Times*. "A voice emerges from an American place. It's got humor, sadness and a fresh and touching rhythm that tell of the loneliness and secrets of life...[a] poetic, haunting play." –*NY Post*. [3M, 1W] ISBN: 0-8222-1850-X

★ **WONDER OF THE WORLD by David Lindsay-Abaire.** A madcap picaresque involving Niagara Falls, a lonely tour-boat captain, a pair of bickering private detectives and a husband's dirty little secret. "Exceedingly whimsical and playfully wicked. Winning and genial. A top-drawer production." –*NY Times*. "Full frontal lunacy is on display. A most assuredly fresh and hilarious tragicomedy of marital discord run amok...absolutely hysterical..." –*Variety*. [3M, 4W (doubling)] ISBN: 0-8222-1863-1

★ **QED by Peter Parnell.** Nobel Prize-winning physicist and all-around genius Richard Feynman holds forth with captivating wit and wisdom in this fascinating biographical play that originally starred Alan Alda. "QED is a seductive mix of science, human affections, moral courage, and comic eccentricity. It reflects on, among other things, death, the absence of God, travel to an unexplored country, the pleasures of drumming, and the need to know and understand." –*NY Magazine*. "Its rhythms correspond to the way that people—even geniuses—approach and avoid highly emotional issues, and it portrays Feynman with affection and awe." –*The New Yorker*. [1M, 1W] ISBN: 0-8222-1924-7

★ **UNWRAP YOUR CANDY by Doug Wright.** Alternately chilling and hilarious, this deliciously macabre collection of four bedtime tales for adults is guaranteed to keep you awake for nights on end. "Engaging and intellectually satisfying...a treat to watch." –*NY Times*. "Fiendishly clever. Mordantly funny and chilling. Doug Wright teases, freezes and zaps us." –*Village Voice*. "Four bite-size plays that bite back." –*Variety*. [flexible casting] ISBN: 0-8222-1871-2

★ **FURTHER THAN THE FURTHEST THING by Zinnie Harris.** On a remote island in the middle of the Atlantic secrets are buried. When the outside world comes calling, the islanders find their world blown apart from the inside as well as beyond. "Harris winningly produces an intimate and poetic, as well as political, family saga." –*Independent (London)*. "Harris' enthralling adventure of a play marks a departure from stale, well-furrowed theatrical terrain." –*Evening Standard (London)*. [3M, 2W] ISBN: 0-8222-1874-7

★ **THE DESIGNATED MOURNER by Wallace Shawn.** The story of three people living in a country where what sort of books people like to read and how they choose to amuse themselves becomes both firmly personal and unexpectedly entangled with questions of survival. "This is a playwright who does not just tell you what it is like to be arrested at night by goons or to fall morally apart and become an aimless yet weirdly contented ghost yourself. He has the originality to make you feel it." –*Times (London)*. "A fascinating play with beautiful passages of writing..." –*Variety*. [2M, 1W] ISBN: 0-8222-1848-8

DRAMATISTS PLAY SERVICE, INC.
440 Park Avenue South, New York, NY 10016 212-683-8960 Fax 212-213-1539
postmaster@dramatists.com www.dramatists.com

NEW PLAYS

★ **SHEL'S SHORTS by Shel Silverstein.** Lauded poet, songwriter and author of children's books, the incomparable Shel Silverstein's short plays are deeply infused with the same wicked sense of humor that made him famous. "...[a] childlike honesty and twisted sense of humor." *–Boston Herald.* "...terse dialogue and an absurdity laced with a tang of dread give [*Shel's Shorts*] more than a trace of Samuel Beckett's comic existentialism." *–Boston Phoenix.* [flexible casting] ISBN: 0-8222-1897-6

★ **AN ADULT EVENING OF SHEL SILVERSTEIN by Shel Silverstein.** Welcome to the darkly comic world of Shel Silverstein, a world where nothing is as it seems and where the most innocent conversation can turn menacing in an instant. These ten imaginative plays vary widely in content, but the style is unmistakable. "...[*An Adult Evening*] shows off Silverstein's virtuosic gift for wordplay...[and] sends the audience out...with a clear appreciation of human nature as perverse and laughable." *–NY Times.* [flexible casting] ISBN: 0-8222-1873-9

★ **WHERE'S MY MONEY? by John Patrick Shanley.** A caustic and sardonic vivisection of the institution of marriage, laced with the author's inimitable razor-sharp wit. "...Shanley's gift for acid-laced one-liners and emotionally tumescent exchanges is certainly potent..." *–Variety.* "...lively, smart, occasionally scary and rich in reverse wisdom." *–NY Times.* [3M, 3W] ISBN: 0-8222-1865-8

★ **A FEW STOUT INDIVIDUALS by John Guare.** A wonderfully screwy comedy-drama that figures Ulysses S. Grant in the throes of writing his memoirs, surrounded by a cast of fantastical characters, including the Emperor and Empress of Japan, the opera star Adelina Patti and Mark Twain. "Guare's smarts, passion and creativity skyrocket to awesome heights..." *–Star Ledger.* "...precisely the kind of good new play that you might call an everyday miracle...every minute of it is fresh and newly alive..." *–Village Voice.* [10M, 3W] ISBN: 0-8222-1907-7

★ **BREATH, BOOM by Kia Corthron.** A look at fourteen years in the life of Prix, a Bronx native, from her ruthless girl-gang leadership at sixteen through her coming to maturity at thirty. "...vivid world, believable and eye-opening, a place worthy of a dramatic visit, where no one would want to live but many have to." *–NY Times.* "...rich with humor, terse vernacular strength and gritty detail..." *–Variety.* [1M, 9W] ISBN: 0-8222-1849-6

★ **THE LATE HENRY MOSS by Sam Shepard.** Two antagonistic brothers, Ray and Earl, are brought together after their father, Henry Moss, is found dead in his seedy New Mexico home in this classic Shepard tale. "...His singular gift has been for building mysteries out of the ordinary ingredients of American family life..." *–NY Times.* "...rich moments ...Shepard finds gold." *–LA Times.* [7M, 1W] ISBN: 0-8222-1858-5

★ **THE CARPETBAGGER'S CHILDREN by Horton Foote.** One family's history spanning from the Civil War to WWII is recounted by three sisters in evocative, intertwining monologues. "...bittersweet music—[a] rhapsody of ambivalence...in its modest, garrulous way...theatrically daring." *–The New Yorker.* [3W] ISBN: 0-8222-1843-7

★ **THE NINA VARIATIONS by Steven Dietz.** In this funny, fierce and heartbreaking homage to *The Seagull*, Dietz puts Chekhov's star-crossed lovers in a room and doesn't let them out. "A perfect little jewel of a play..." *–Shepherdstown Chronicle.* "...a delightful revelation of a writer at play; and also an odd, haunting, moving theater piece of lingering beauty." *–Eastside Journal (Seattle).* [1M, 1W (flexible casting)] ISBN: 0-8222-1891-7

DRAMATISTS PLAY SERVICE, INC.
440 Park Avenue South, New York, NY 10016 212-683-8960 Fax 212-213-1539
postmaster@dramatists.com www.dramatists.com